BRAIN
Training & Conversion

L E A P Learning Empowerment & Achieving Potential

ISBN 978-93-81115-69-5

First published in 2011 by Leadstart
A brand of One Point Six Technologies Private Limited
Unit no. 26, Ground Floor, A1, Shram Safalya,
Wadala Truck Terminal Road, Near Post Office,
Antop Hill, Mumbai -400037.
Email:info@leadstartcorp.com
www.leadstartcorp.com

Marketed & Distributed in India by Unbound Script
2/41, Ansari Road, Darayaganj, Delhi - 110002

EDITORS OF LEADSTART

The Editors of Leadstart are a team of passionate literary enthusiasts with a creative and progressive focus. Our team includes distinguished authors, researchers, contributors, in-house editors, and writing talent from around the world. Many literary projects require a diverse team rather than a single author to write or update the book. These projects often involve cases where the original author is unable to continue, whether because they are unavailable or no longer with us. Our work thus spans a range of content, from original writings to thoughtfully abridged classics, updated editions, and translations.

ABOUT THE LEAP SERIES

The LEAP series of books has been conceived as a tool of empowerment for every individual to achieve their full potential.

There are certain aspirations that every person in the world shares. We all want to be happy. We all want to lead fulfilling lives. We all want to find our soulmate. We all want a job we love doing. We all want good friends who will share our joy and sorrow. We all want to believe that there is a purpose to our lives.

While the commonality of these goals spans the globe, their achievement is entirely individual. Each person possesses a unique and mixed gift of strengths and weaknesses, special talents and handicaps. To focus our individual lives on all that is positive within us, all that is possible for us to do, to be and to achieve, we need to take conscious steps towards it. The empowerment of our lives is an individual pursuit. The decisions are yours. The action is yours. To do the very best with what one has been given – that is the ultimate achievement of a life well lived.

You Are You
First, we must recognise ourselves and accept our particular basket of capabilities. Nobody is the same. Nor is it necessary to be like someone else.

Find Your Horizons
Once we are at peace with the composition of our own individuality, we can set out to enhance our capabilities in order to achieve full potential as an individual. We can utilise all the teaching around us to stretch our talents to the fullest extent to achieve worthwhile goals.

Cap The Leak
Once we recognise our potential, we can work to minimise the influence and impact of our weak points to allow the strengths to shine in everything we do.

Row Your Boat
Every day is part of the journey. Sometimes you win the day. Sometimes the day is lost. But you keep rowing towards the shore, towards your goals. In India, it is called sadhana. That special power within you drives you to achieve what you have set yourself to do.

The LEAP series teaches methods of individual empowerment.

ﻩﻩ

CONTENTS

INTRODUCTION

Modern life places the mind under a kind of pressure that previous generations could barely imagine. At any moment, you may be trying to balance financial worries, work pressures, school expectations, global news that feels overwhelming, the constant comparison created by social media, and the digital noise of notifications that never truly stop. Even when nothing catastrophic is happening, the steady pull of daily stressors keeps your nervous system on alert. Over time, this creates a mental environment where memory, clarity, and focus begin to suffer.

Stress does not always arrive dramatically. It often shows up, building layer by layer until your thoughts feel scattered and your mind feels heavy. When the brain is constantly bracing itself, it struggles to store new information or retrieve old memories. You may notice that you forget names more easily, misplace items, reread the same page without absorbing it, or walk into a room and instantly lose track of what you came for. This is not a sign that something is wrong with you. It is a sign that your mind is protecting itself by diverting energy to survival rather than recall.

The brain is an extraordinary organ, responsible not only for thinking and learning but also for regulating heart rate, temperature, hormones, digestion, and the entire nervous system. It works tirelessly, even when you sleep. For it to operate at its full potential, it needs a state of calm, safety, and internal balance. When the mind is tense, it becomes much harder for neural connections to form. When the mind relaxes, those same pathways open, strengthen, and connect with ease.

This is why relaxation is not a luxury or indulgence. It is a requirement for a healthy mind. When you create space for stillness, the brain begins to repair itself. Stress hormones decrease. The nervous system settles. And memory returns to a more natural rhythm. Even a few minutes of calm breathing or a moment of silence can begin to shift the entire internal landscape of your thoughts.

Creating a Supportive Environment for the Brain

One of the simplest ways to help your memory is to shape your surroundings so they feel stable and soothing. The brain thrives in environments that offer clarity, and comfort. Soft lighting, reduced clutter, slow music, or even a clean work surface can make a surprising difference. These sensory cues tell your nervous system that it is safe to focus. When the mind is not bracing for disruption, it can finally pay attention.

Creating this kind of space does not require expensive tools. It can be as simple as dimming a bright lamp, clearing a small corner of your desk, or stepping away from overstimulating environments for a few minutes each day. Over time, the brain begins to associate these cues with ease and readiness for learning, much like a familiar routine primes muscles before exercise.

The Role of Relaxation Devices and Technology

In recent years, researchers and therapists have been experimenting with tools designed to help the brain relax more deeply. These devices use sound frequencies, gentle pulses, or calming rhythms to guide the mind into states where stress loosens and clarity rises. While not necessary for everyone, these technologies show promise for individuals whose minds feel stuck in constant tension. Think of them as modern forms of guided relaxation that help the brain step out of overdrive.

Even without devices, traditional techniques such as deep breathing, meditation, progressive muscle relaxation, and guided imagery offer similar benefits. They slow the heart rate, reduce cortisol, and allow the mind to shift from survival mode into learning mode. The calmer the internal environment, the more easily your memory begins to organise itself again.

Your Body and Your Brain: One System, Not Two

It is impossible to separate the health of the body from the clarity of the mind. The brain is part of the central nervous system, and anything that affects your posture, breathing, or level of physical tension also affects your cognitive performance. When the neck and shoulders are tight, when breathing is shallow, or when the spine is strained, the brain receives less oxygen and begins to fatigue more quickly. You might notice this as fogginess, irritability, or difficulty concentrating.

Supporting your body with rest, gentle movement, hydration, and better posture directly supports your memory. Even small changes matter. A short stretch, a slow walk, or a few deep breaths can refresh your mind more effectively than pushing through exhaustion. The brain thinks more clearly when the body feels grounded.

Why Stress Disrupts Memory

One of the most fascinating things about memory is that most of it lives in the subconscious mind. It stores thousands of facts, experiences, and impressions that you may not be consciously aware of. However, stress interferes with the bridge between the conscious and subconscious. When stress rises, access to stored information becomes inconsistent. You may know a fact perfectly well but find that it slips away the moment you need it.

This is why you might remember a detail hours later, long after the stressful moment has passed. Your memory did not fail. Your mind simply could not retrieve the information while it was busy managing stress.

Relaxation restores that bridge. When the mind is calm, recall becomes smooth and intuitive. You can piece together ideas, remember names, solve problems, and think more creatively. Calm opens the door to clarity.

How Relaxation Helps Memory Return

Think of relaxation as resetting the nervous system. When the mind feels steady, your thoughts fall into place. Memories that felt lost begin to surface again. You remember where you kept your keys, what you intended to say, or the name that felt impossible to recall moments earlier.

This is not magic. It is simply biology. A relaxed brain works better.

Over time, regular relaxation creates deeper, more stable memory pathways. It teaches the mind that it does not need to react to every noise, message, or thought with urgency. It trains the nervous system to stay steady, even in challenging situations. And as this internal balance grows, your memory becomes sharper, faster, and more dependable.

The Heart of It All

If you want better recall, stronger focus, and clearer thinking, give your brain what it needs most: rest, balance, and ease. When your inner world settles, your memory rises to meet you with strength and clarity. And in that stillness, the mind you have been struggling to support finally begins to support you in return.

ꙮ

1

HOW THE BRAIN FUNCTIONS & ITS INTRICATE NATURE

You've probably heard the legendary tale of Archimedes, the ancient Greek scientist who had one of the most famous "aha!" moments in history. The king suspected that his gold crown wasn't pure, but how could Archimedes prove it without melting it down? He puzzled over it until one day, stepping into his bath, he noticed the water rising. That's when it hit him: the amount of water displaced could tell him the volume of the crown! With this breakthrough, he could figure out if it was made of pure gold or not. So excited was he that he leapt out of the tub and ran through the streets shouting "Eureka!", which means "I found it!"

But here's the real question: what does this have to do with our brains? A lot.

Archimedes' story is a perfect example of how a single, seemingly random event can spark a powerful chain reaction in the brain. Just one simple observation, bathwater rising, triggered a brilliant scientific insight. It makes you wonder: why does the brain respond like this? Why does one tiny moment cause an explosion of inspiration in one person, while another might feel nothing at all, or worse, get totally overwhelmed?

To understand this, we need to take a peek into the wild, wonderful world inside our heads.

The brain isn't just a grey lump of tissue, it's a living, breathing, energy-swigging party of activity. It's what scientists call an open system, meaning it's constantly interacting with the world around it. It's never in a steady state; instead, it's buzzing with chemical and electrical signals, pulsing in waves, and throwing a nonstop disco inside your skull.

And here's the kicker: it's incredibly sensitive. Think of it like a super high-tech orchestra where even the tiniest change, like two of your billions of brain cells changing their behaviour, can throw the whole thing into chaos or, just maybe, spark genius.

This is why that one red cape, flashing light, or bathtub moment can set off a chain reaction in the brain that leads to a brand-new idea. Your brain is always looking, always listening, always connecting dots in the background, and now and then, something clicks.

So the next time you have your own "Eureka!" moment, maybe in the shower, on a walk, or while eating cereal, remember Archimedes, and thank your brilliant, buzzing brain for being the magical, unpredictable machine that it is.

Why the complexity of the brain makes it a prime candidate for enhancement:

Because the brain is such a beautifully complex and advanced system, scientists have turned to some pretty fascinating ideas to understand how it works. One of the coolest concepts out there is something called a *dissipative structure*. Sounds fancy, right? But stick with me, it's not as intimidating as it sounds.

Think of a dissipative structure as something that thrives in chaos. It doesn't sit still or stay the same, it's constantly exchanging energy with the world around it. It *needs* this flow of energy to keep functioning and growing. And guess what? Your brain is one of those structures!

What this means is that, with just the right kind of energy input, say, a powerful idea, an emotional jolt, or even a surprise twist in your daily routine, the brain can become a bit unstable. Not in a bad way, though. It's more like shaking a kaleidoscope. At first, it's all jumbled, but then... click! A brand-new, beautiful pattern appears.

That's how scientists believe the brain sometimes works: internal shifts and fluctuations build up until, boom, a moment of transformation. The brain reorganises itself into a new state that's more connected, more complex, and more in tune with everything it's been taking in. In other words, it levels up.

So those sudden leaps in thinking, those moments when things "just make sense," might be your brain rearranging itself into something even better than before.

Augmenting the potential of the brain through machines:

Let's talk about brain enhancement machines. Yep, real devices that aim to supercharge your mind by giving it an extra boost of energy. Sounds like science fiction? It's not. These gadgets use things like flashing lights, rhythmic sound waves, electromagnetic fields, or even total sensory isolation (think floating in a tank, cut off from all external input) to gently nudge the brain out of its usual rhythm.

The idea? By increasing the brain's energy flow, we might be able to stir up its natural fluctuations and push it into a brand-new state, one that's more ordered, more connected, and quite possibly... smarter. Like tuning a radio and suddenly landing on a clearer, richer signal.

So here's the big question: can these machines *unlock* the brain's self-organising power? Can they help the brain evolve into a more complex, more coherent, higher-functioning version of itself? If the answer is yes, then we're not just talking about fancy tech, we're talking about tools with the power to revolutionise how we think, learn, and even *be*.

Now, here's something scientists already know: the brain *needs* a steady stream of energy and fresh experiences to grow and stay healthy. We see this in how babies develop. Infants raised in environments full of colours, sounds, love, and stimulation tend to grow faster, mentally and emotionally, than those who don't get that input. It's like the brain is a sponge, but it needs water to stay soft and absorbent.

Normally, the brain handles small doses of input just fine, it takes in new ideas, events, or sensations without needing to rearrange itself. But when the stimulation reaches a certain intensity, something fascinating happens. The brain can't just carry on as usual. Its internal patterns start to wobble and shake, and eventually, it snaps into a brand-new mode of understanding. At first, everything feels confusing, like the pieces don't fit. But then suddenly, a new picture forms. A new way of seeing the world. A breakthrough. The brain has restructured itself into a smarter, sharper, more connected version.

ꕥ

2

THE CENTRAL NERVOUS SYSTEM

The idea of enhancing the brain used to feel like science fiction, but today it is part of everyday conversation. People explore memory apps, cognitive training programs, and digital exercises that promise sharper thinking. The newest generation of brain enhancement software goes even further. Instead of simply offering puzzles or concentration drills, these programs draw from fields such as kinaesthetics, behavioural psychology, neuroplasticity, and even sociocultural research. Some are designed to adapt to your personality style or your cultural environment. Others try to identify your learning patterns so they can personalise training around them. These tools are clever, and in many cases, they are genuinely helpful. But they raise an important question that often goes unasked: when do these programs stop being simple mental exercises and begin influencing the physical systems that allow memory and cognition to exist in the first place?

To answer that question, we need to look beneath the surface of thought and into the central nervous system. The CNS is not just a supportive structure. It is the foundation on which all memory, attention, coordination, and consciousness depend. When this system becomes strained, blocked, or disrupted, the consequences are immediate and noticeable. People may experience headaches or dizziness, which are early signs that the nervous system is struggling to maintain balance. Others may notice changes in coordination, episodes of confusion, unexpected fatigue, or memory fog that seems to appear out of nowhere. These symptoms are not isolated. They reflect a deeper disruption in the brain's communication network.

The central nervous system functions like a vast electrical grid that connects every physical and cognitive process in the body. It includes the brain, the spinal cord, and the complex network of nerves that branch outward to every organ and limb. When all parts of this system are aligned and working together, information flows smoothly. Messages travel from one neuron to another with clarity. Reflexes respond promptly. Memory forms and retrieves more easily because the pathways that carry information are unobstructed. When the system is compromised, the flow of communication becomes distorted, and the entire experience of thinking, moving, remembering, and reacting can shift.

One of the most important and often overlooked parts of this system is the spinal column. Most people think of the spine as a simple structural support. In reality, it is the protective casing for the spinal cord, which is the main highway of the central nervous system. Every message sent from the brain to the body passes through this channel. If the spine becomes misaligned or strained, the nervous system experiences something similar to a blocked road. Signals that once moved freely become delayed, confused, or weakened. This is why issues in the spine can lead to symptoms that seem unrelated at first, such as muscle weakness, visual disturbances, changes in reflexes, or sudden problems with balance.

Inside the brain itself, the consequences of nervous system strain can affect every major region. The four lobes of the brain support memory, movement, emotional processing, language, decision making, and sensory awareness. The thalamus filters information and decides what reaches conscious awareness. The hypothalamus regulates hormones, temperature, appetite, sleep cycles, and emotional responses. The brain stem controls vital reflexes that keep you alive, such as breathing and heart rate. The cerebellum manages coordination and balance. The cranial nerves support vision, facial movement, swallowing, hearing, and speech. When the nervous system becomes overwhelmed or misaligned, any of these functions can be affected. What looks like a memory problem can actually be a nervous system problem that has impacted the regions responsible for recall.

When the CNS begins to send irregular signals, the symptoms can seem strange or unpredictable. People may notice their pupils responding irregularly to light. Others may experience numbness or tingling, or an unusual feeling of weakness when trying to lift an object. Reflexes may change, and automatic functions such as swallowing, blinking, or coughing may slow down. These changes are not random. They show that the communication lines between the brain and body have been interrupted, and the nervous system is trying to compensate.

Understanding this deeper relationship between the nervous system and cognitive function creates a more holistic view of memory enhancement. True cognitive improvement cannot come only from apps, mental exercises, or digital tools, even though these can be useful. Real enhancement requires supporting the physical systems that allow the brain to function. When the spine is aligned, when the nervous system is balanced, and when the brain's pathways are clear, memory becomes sharper because the system that carries information is operating without interference.

The future of cognitive enhancement will likely combine mental training, physical support, and nervous system care. This might include therapies that improve spinal alignment, gentle forms of bodywork that reduce tension in the nervous system, or advanced devices that help regulate stress and promote relaxation. It may involve digital programs that work alongside physical techniques so that both mind and body can strengthen together. When the brain, spinal cord, and nervous system are treated as one continuous system, the approach to memory shifts from quick tricks to long-term strength.

The takeaway is clear. If you want a better memory, a sharper mind, or more mental energy, you must look beyond the surface. Your brain cannot perform well if the system that carries its signals is strained. Support the spine. Reduce tension in the nervous system. Give the body the alignment it needs for the brain to function at its best. When the communication lines of the CNS flow smoothly, memory improves not because you forced it, but because you finally allowed the entire system to work the way it was designed.

ഉരു

3

SCIENTIFIC BREAKTHROUGHS

Scientists have been making some pretty exciting discoveries about how the brain grows, how it ages, and, perhaps most fascinating of all, how it can *regenerate* itself. These findings are shedding new light on one of our most mysterious abilities: learning. Or, in some cases, why learning doesn't happen the way we expect it to.

By diving into this research, scientists are piecing together a bigger picture of how the brain functions daily. The more they understand about these natural processes, what boosts learning, what slows it down, and how the brain changes over time, the closer they get to figuring out how to *influence* them.

And here's where it gets really interesting: all this knowledge isn't just meant for lab reports. The ultimate goal is to take these discoveries and turn them into real-world tools, apps, therapies, training programs, and maybe even brain-enhancing tech, that everyday people can use to learn better, stay mentally sharp longer, and tap into the brain's incredible ability to adapt and grow.

Brain growth and its relation to brain enhancement:

For a long time, scientists believed that the size of your brain was pretty much written in your DNA, something you inherited from your parents, like your eye colour or height. But it turns out that's not the whole story.

Recent research has flipped this old assumption on its head. Studies looking into the heredity of brain size have revealed something pretty amazing: your environment can *grow* your brain.

Specifically, scientists found that when people (and even animals) are exposed to what's called an *enriched environment*, a setting full of stimulation, learning opportunities, sensory input, and even social interaction, the brain physically responds. We're talking real, measurable changes here: increased brain weight, more brain cells, a thicker cortex (that's the brain's thinking cap), and even *larger neurons*. Yes, the actual brain cells themselves grew!

Even more impressively, the number of certain specialised brain cells went up, too. So in short, the brain isn't just a static organ, it's dynamic, flexible, and capable of growth when given the right kind of input.

The ageing of the human brain and its relation to brain enhancement:

For a long time, scientists believed that the size of your brain was pretty much written in your DNA, something you inherited from your parents, like your eye colour or height. But it turns out that's not the whole story.

Recent research has flipped this old assumption on its head. Studies looking into the heredity of brain size have revealed something pretty amazing: your environment can *grow* your brain.

Specifically, scientists found that when people (and even animals) are exposed to what's called an *enriched environment*, a setting full of stimulation, learning opportunities, sensory input, and even social interaction, the brain physically responds. We're talking real, measurable changes here: increased brain weight, more brain cells, a thicker cortex (that's the brain's thinking cap), and even *larger neurons*. Yes, the actual brain cells themselves grew!

Even more impressively, the number of certain specialised brain cells went up too. So in short, the brain isn't just a static organ, it's dynamic, flexible, and totally capable of growth when given the right kind of input.

The regenerative abilities of the brain and their relation to brain enhancement:

For decades, scientists believed one of the brain's most unfortunate truths: unlike other cells in the body, brain cells, called neurons, couldn't regenerate. That meant the brain you had by the age of two was the brain you'd have for life. Lose neurons? Too bad, they were gone for good. It painted a pretty bleak picture: as we aged, we were supposedly doomed to slowly lose brain cells, with no chance of ever getting them back.

But here's the exciting twist, this long-standing belief has been proven wrong. Around two decades ago, groundbreaking studies revealed something incredible: under the right conditions, the brain *can* regenerate. Neurons aren't as helpless as we once thought. In fact, with the right kind of stimulation and support, the brain can heal itself, even generating new brain cells, just like skin grows back after a cut.

This discovery was a game-changer. It means the brain isn't just a fragile organ in slow decline, it's resilient, adaptive, and capable of bouncing back. New scientific research shows the brain is far more powerful than we ever imagined.

Even better? Once you understand how your brain works, its functions, its current state, and how it responds to different stimuli, you can start *training* it. Using techniques developed over the past few decades, people can now tap into the brain's own power to improve focus, boost memory, manage emotions, and even support healing and growth.

It's like upgrading your mental software, only now, the hardware can upgrade itself too.

Brain synchronisation and dual inductions – their roles in the process of brain enhancement

One of the coolest revelations in brain science came from studies on brain lateralisation, the idea that the right and left sides of our brain operate differently, almost like they each have their own personality. The left side tends to be logical and analytical, while the right side is more creative and intuitive. What surprised scientists was that we typically use just *one side at a time*, with dominance flipping back and forth depending on what we're doing.

This led to the development of a fascinating technique called dual inductions. So, what's that? Imagine lying down, putting on a pair of headphones, and hearing two calming voices, one in your left ear, one in your right, each guiding you gently into a deeply relaxed, trance-like state. It might sound strange at first, almost spooky, like an echo bouncing inside your head. But that's the magic of dual inductions: they're designed to engage both sides of your brain at once.

At first, this might feel a bit overwhelming or unfamiliar. After all, we're not used to working both hemispheres of our brain simultaneously. But here's the exciting part: when you do, amazing things start to happen. Memory sharpens, focus improves, and the brain's ability to process information increases dramatically. It's like giving your mind a full-body workout.

Today's brain enhancement programs are using this technique not just for relaxation, but to boost brain performance in powerful ways. And once you get past that initial weirdness, many people find dual inductions soothing, even transformative.

The electrochemical brain and how it relates to the process of brain enhancement:

Scientists now agree on something pretty mind-blowing: every mental state you experience, whether it's joy, sadness, deep focus, or daydreaming, is tied to a unique pattern of electrical and chemical activity in your brain. Think of your brain like a symphony of signals, constantly firing in different rhythms and patterns depending on what you're feeling or thinking.

Even more fascinating? These patterns aren't fixed. They can be shaped and changed by external stimuli, things like light, sound, physical movement, and even electromagnetic fields.

This is where technology steps in. Scientists have developed mechanical devices that can deliver precise stimuli to specific areas of the brain, almost like tuning an instrument. With these tools, it's now possible to reliably guide your brain into very specific states: euphoria, deep relaxation, vivid daydreams, and even the recall of long-forgotten memories.

And that's just the beginning. These devices can help unlock deep concentration, stimulate sexual excitement, ignite bursts of creativity, or stir up vivid memories from the past. It's not science fiction, it's a growing field of brain science that's opening doors to experiences once thought to be purely internal or uncontrollable.

In short, with the right tools and a bit of know-how, you can *choose* your state of mind.

ഇരു

4

ACCESSING OUR POTENTIAL

Brain enhancement programs are all about unlocking the hidden superpowers we all carry inside us. These tools don't give you anything new, they just help you tap into what's already there. By combining the power of suggestion with soothing voices, calming visuals, and ambient sounds, these programs guide people into a relaxed state where focus sharpens, memory improves, and motivation naturally rises.

It's kind of like flipping a mental switch. As the background music plays, filled with soft, repetitive tones and subtle electrical sounds, it gently quiets the noise in your head. Once the mind relaxes, something amazing happens: the brain becomes more efficient, better at sending and receiving signals between nerve cells. Studies show that when the body and mind are calm, memory improves, focus deepens, and creativity gets a boost.

The whole process is a bit like optimising a computer. Think of your brain as incredibly powerful software. In programming, developers write the cleanest, most efficient lines of code possible to get the fastest results. Brain enhancement programs do something similar: they "streamline" the brain's processes using optimised techniques and targeted instructions. The goal? To help you learn faster, think clearly, and develop abilities that have been lying dormant.

But there's a catch, you have to show up and do the work. These programs are most effective when users follow the guided sessions closely and stick to the strategies provided. It's not magic. It's a smart, science-based method to help your brain function like the high-performance machine it is.

Role of brain enhancement machines in optimising peak experiences:

Brain machines are helping people unlock one of the most powerful secrets of the human mind: our natural ability to learn and grow simply by increasing brain coherence, that is, getting the brain's different parts to work in sync. When that happens, something magical unfolds: people start experiencing what psychologists call "peak experiences."

These are those unforgettable moments when everything just *clicks*. You feel fully alive, totally present, and deeply fulfilled. It could happen when you're making love, gazing at your sleeping child, getting lost in a beautiful painting, or solving a complex problem. These moments feel so good, so *right*, that most of us would love to have them as often as possible.

One of the strongest forces driving human behaviour is the desire to experience these peaks. We chase them through love, sex, success, art, money, power, and wisdom. Sadly, we often take wrong turns, drugs, toxic relationships, burnout careers, hoping they'll lead to lasting highs. They rarely do.

Over the centuries, people have created all kinds of methods to spark peak states, meditation, yoga, prayer, fasting, psychedelics, and rituals. While some of these paths are powerful and proven, they often require discipline, patience, and years of practice. Not a great fit for a fast-paced world hungry for instant results.

The problem? Most shortcuts people try, materialism, shallow spirituality, or mindless distractions, end up backfiring. When they don't deliver the bliss they promised, people start doubting the very *existence* of peak experiences. The result is cynicism: "It's all fake," they say, dismissing joy, creativity, and higher states of awareness as unrealistic fluff for the overly sensitive.

But here's the real question: Can we intentionally create these experiences? Can we guide ourselves into higher mental states on purpose?

The answer may lie in understanding the flow state, that feeling of total immersion when you're doing something challenging yet enjoyable. Flow isn't always comfortable, but it's energising. It's when people do their best thinking, learning, and creating.

Activities like painting, playing music, sports, or deep study all create flow. And brain machines aim to replicate the brainwaves and patterns that lead to that state, without the long wait or the side effects.

By helping the brain enter a state of deep relaxation and focused energy, these technologies open the door to more frequent peak experiences. And that's not just exciting, it's empowering. Because once you understand that *you* can control your mind, shape your experiences, and awaken your potential, the search becomes a journey of joy, not frustration.

Photic brain enhancement programmes:

One of the coolest tools making waves in modern brain enhancement programs is something called photic stimulation, and trust us, it's as sci-fi as it sounds!

Photic stimulators use flashing lights, yep, lights, to "fascinate" your brain into shifting gears. These lights flicker in rhythmic pulses, matching the frequencies of your brainwaves. It's like a light show designed *just* for your mind. Some programs use screens where lights dance in sync, while others use special LED goggles that flash light patterns directly over your closed eyes.

But, important note, if you have a history of seizures or epilepsy, these gadgets should be avoided. Safety first.

So, how does it work? Think of it like this: flashing lights, like the ones on Christmas trees or at concerts, often mesmerise us, right? They can make you feel oddly relaxed or "zoned out." Brain-enhancement tech takes that same principle and turns it up a notch with precise photic patterns to guide your brain into specific states, like deep relaxation, focused attention, or even creative flow.

When paired with sound (like calming tones or music), these visual pulses create a supercharged sensory experience. Even with your eyes closed, the light travels through your eyelids, gently stimulating the cortex and other parts of your brain tied to memory, creativity, and mood. It's like giving your brain a little light massage.

Now, here's where it gets even more fascinating: colour matters, a lot. Different colours trigger different emotional and physical responses:

- **Red** = Energising. It can boost energy levels but also trigger stress or anxiety, so it's never used alone.
- **Brown** = Soothing. Calms irritability, stress, and low moods.
- **Orange** = Sparks creativity. Great when you're in a rut.
- **Yellow** = Boosts insight and creative thinking, but be careful, it can also stir up frustration if overused.
- **Green** = Super peaceful. Think of nature, calm, and restoring.
- **Blue** = Deeply relaxing. It soothes the soul, helps breathing slow down, and even promotes healthy metabolism and brain growth.
- **Indigo** = Pain relief and emotional balance.
- **Violet** = Encourages spiritual awareness and calms cravings.
- **White** = Helps with visualisation and imagination.

These colours aren't just pretty, they're purposeful. Used in specific combinations, they help guide your mind toward a desired state: calm, creative, alert, or inspired.

So whether you're trying to spark genius ideas or just chill after a long day, photic stimulation offers a gentle, tech-assisted path to a better state of mind. Think of it as a brain tune-up, no wires, no pills, just light and colour doing their thing.

ᘓᘐ

5

EVOLVING PERSPECTIVES

There was a time when people believed that intelligence could be measured simply by weighing a brain. If a person had a larger brain, they were assumed to be smarter, more capable, and more evolved. It seemed logical enough on the surface, but when scientists began examining brains after death, they discovered something that rewrote the story entirely. Some individuals who had struggled intellectually had surprisingly large brains, while others who had produced extraordinary ideas and creative breakthroughs had brains that were smaller than average. The early theory fell apart, and with it went the idea that intelligence was a simple matter of biological size. What remained was the real mystery: if size was not the source of intelligence, what was?

For decades, the scientific community clung to another rigid belief. Intelligence was seen as something fixed, a genetic inheritance that could not be changed. You were either born bright or born average, and nothing you did in life could meaningfully expand your cognitive abilities. Even more limiting was the belief that the brain's neurons were like a nonrenewable resource. You had the maximum at birth, and every loss was permanent. This idea created an entire cultural attitude based on limitation. People who struggled with memory or learning thought they were simply unlucky. People who grew older believed that decline was inevitable. The brain was a static organ rather than a living, evolving system.

Science eventually proved how inaccurate those assumptions were. Modern neuroscience has shown that the brain is dynamic, responsive, and profoundly adaptable. It can form new connections throughout life. It can reorganise networks after injury. Under the right conditions, it can even generate new neurons. With practice, stimulation, challenge, and repetition, the brain changes physically. Every skill you learn, every habit you build, every memory you form leaves a structural fingerprint on the brain. This discovery transformed our understanding of intelligence. It shifted the narrative from limitation to possibility. Intelligence was no longer something you were handed at birth. It was something you could cultivate.

This shift laid the foundation for technologies designed to enhance cognitive performance. Brain enhancement machines, once the stuff of science fiction, now sit at the intersection of neuroscience and everyday life. They are built on the idea that the brain responds to sensory stimulation, electrical patterns, rhythmic sound, and guided cognitive tasks. Just as the muscles in your body react to resistance training, the neural pathways in your brain respond to deliberate cognitive stimulation. These devices act like gym equipment for the mind, offering structured exercises that strengthen attention, stimulate memory, and increase cognitive flexibility. They are tools, not miracles, but when used thoughtfully, they can create meaningful changes in how the brain functions.

To appreciate how far this field has come, it helps to look at its beginnings. Early machines associated with the brain were purely diagnostic. Electroencephalography records brain waves to detect disorders such as epilepsy. CAT scans allowed doctors to view internal structures without surgery. Electrical stimulation can treat chronic pain or severe depression. These technologies were powerful but limited to identifying or reducing harm. They were never meant to help healthy people improve their cognitive abilities. The idea of using machines to upgrade normal brain performance would have sounded strange, even irresponsible.

But as researchers examined EEG readings more closely, they saw something unexpected. The brain's electrical activity was profoundly influenced by external stimulation. Stress altered the patterns dramatically. Certain sound frequencies calmed the nervous system. Specific rhythms improved attention. This realisation opened the door to a revolutionary idea. If the brain responds so clearly to external signals, could carefully designed sensory input enhance cognitive performance? Could sound, light, and guided instruction help the brain learn faster and think more clearly?

The answer, according to early experiments, was yes. Students exposed to structured music sessions during learning performed better on memory tasks. Their concentration improved, their recall strengthened, and their overall mental performance rose. Rhythmic sound created predictable neural patterns that made the brain more receptive and stable. Voice-guided learning sessions supported comprehension and retention. These discoveries showed that the brain was not just reacting passively. It was adapting. It was learning how to learn more effectively.

This new knowledge inspired the development of modern neuro-enhancement programs. Today, machines and digital tools are not just treating illness. They are being studied as potential ways to help healthy individuals sharpen their cognition, improve their emotional stability, and strengthen their memory in ways once thought impossible. Some focus on relaxation and brainwave regulation. Others use carefully designed light patterns to stimulate neural activity. Many rely on targeted audio frequencies that encourage certain states of focus, creativity, or retention. While these tools are not substitutes for sleep, nutrition, movement, or emotional well-being, they add to the growing understanding that the brain can be shaped by deliberate stimulation.

All of this leads to a simple but powerful conclusion. The mind is not a fixed entity that stops growing once childhood ends. It is a living, trainable system that responds to challenge, nourishment, and experience. It can be strengthened in many ways, from the environment you create to the tools you use to the habits you build. Machines alone will not give you a perfect memory, but they represent one piece of a much larger truth. Human potential is not static. With the right support, the brain can continue to evolve across an entire lifetime.

ജ്ഞ

6

INNATE RESPONSES

Electromyography (EMG) might sound like a mouthful, but it's simply a technique used to measure the electrical activity in your muscles. Essentially, it tracks muscle tension. And guess what? Scientists discovered something interesting: a quick session in a flotation tank (that serene space where you float weightlessly) created a deep state of relaxation, meditation, and muscle relaxation. It worked so well that mind machines and other similar devices could rapidly trigger this kind of profound relaxation, too.

The relaxation that these machines induce is almost immediate, and it's incredibly enjoyable. But there's a catch: some of the words used to describe the experience include "instability," "novelty," and "fluctuations." While these terms might sound a little off-putting or mysterious, they highlight a unique process. The experience is fun and refreshing, but can also feel a bit unsettling. But what does all this have to do with deep relaxation?

As humans, we're built to survive and thrive, and we have an evolutionary tool that's helped us do just that: the fight or flight response. This is the body's automatic reaction to perceived threats, think adrenaline pumping through your veins, preparing you to either run or fight. It's a rush that floods the body with energy, making your muscles tense up and your heart race faster. It's a lifesaver when you're faced with a dangerous predator or an emergency.

But here's the twist: while the fight or flight response is a great survival mechanism, it's not ideal for rational thought or clear decision-making. After all, if you're running from a hungry lion, you probably won't be pondering life's deeper questions.

When adrenaline takes over, blood and oxygen flow to the muscles, leaving your brain in a bit of a fog. The result? You might make poor decisions because your body is focused on survival, not critical thinking.

Stress, whether from a looming deadline or personal loss, has a similar effect. Under extreme stress, the ability to think clearly and make decisions takes a serious hit. People facing high-stress situations often find it hard to focus or concentrate, which makes learning and thinking productively even more challenging.

So, how does this relate to relaxation machines? Well, these tools help guide your body and mind away from that fight or flight mode, unlocking the ability to focus and think clearly. Relaxation isn't just about feeling good, it's about giving your brain the space it needs to operate at its full potential. And that's where these technologies shine.

The Relaxation Response: Tapping into the Brain's Power for Peak Performance

Just like the fight or flight response, the body also has an opposite reaction, a kind of "chill-out" mode that helps us relax. While the fight or flight response gets us ready for action, this second system focuses our body's energy inward, promoting relaxation and recovery. When activated, it reduces heart rate, lowers blood pressure, and eases muscle tension. In addition, it boosts the functioning of the gastrointestinal tract and sends more oxygen and blood to the brain. Talk about a brain boost!

This shift in the body's activity also leads to a change in brainwave patterns. Instead of the quick, rapid beta waves that occur when we're focused on the outside world, the brain switches to slower, higher-amplitude alpha and theta waves, the kind of brain activity that's found in states of meditation or deep contemplation. This state of calm is known as the relaxation response (or sometimes the quieting reflex), and it's a natural, innate ability that humans (and mammals in general) have.

Think about it, cats and dogs are perfect examples. They can go from high-energy play to instant relaxation, curling up, yawning, and falling into deep rest. Unfortunately, with the fast pace of modern life and the constant buzz of urban and industrial stressors, many of us have lost the ability to switch off quickly. But don't worry, we've developed techniques to bring back that sweet relaxation state, from meditation to deep breathing to biofeedback.

And here's the good news: Relaxation isn't just about chilling out; it helps you perform better, mentally and physically. Studies consistently show that people who stay cool-headed under pressure or relax during problem-solving tasks tend to perform better. It's not just about avoiding stress, it's about unlocking your full potential.

So, what does it take to tap into this relaxation state? According to research, there are four key components:

- **A constant stimulus** (think soothing music or soft background sounds).
- **A passive attitude** (letting go of distractions and stressors).
- **Decreased muscle tension** (making sure you're in a relaxed, comfortable position).
- **A quiet, calm environment** with minimal external distractions.

Relaxation and Brain Enhancement Machines

Now, here's where it gets exciting: Brain enhancement machines are designed to do just that, trigger relaxation and boost mental performance. Most of these devices provide exactly what's needed to stimulate the relaxation response. Whether it's through lights, sounds, body movements, or electromagnetic fields, these machines offer the constant stimulus that your brain craves.

Users are encouraged to relax, adopt a passive attitude, and find a comfortable posture. With the right environment (quiet and peaceful), the brain can easily slip into that relaxed state, and that's where the magic happens.

Since stress is a major roadblock to mental clarity and focus, and relaxation enhances it, the fact that these devices can quickly induce deep relaxation explains why users often experience improved mental functioning. Whether you're trying to boost your memory, solve a tricky problem, or just de-stress after a long day, brain enhancement tools can provide the perfect environment for optimal mental performance.

Ꟊ

7

SCIENTIFIC USES OF BRAIN ENHANCEMENT

The combination of deep relaxation techniques and innovative brain enhancement methods like white noise, photic stimulators, and electric sound pulses might seem like a futuristic gimmick to some, but in reality, they have been shown to produce tangible, proven results. Far from misleading, these methods have garnered scientific validation through extensive research and have been adopted by schools, universities, and mental health facilities worldwide.

Far from a passing trend, these techniques have demonstrated powerful benefits, especially in the context of learning and cognitive enhancement. Multiple tests have shown that tools like sound, visuals, and light can significantly help relax the mind and facilitate deeper learning. This is why scientists, medical experts, and psychiatrists alike are championing the use of brain enhancement techniques, because they work.

For example, research has consistently demonstrated that these methods result in a notable improvement in students' ability to absorb, process, and recall information. When students were subjected to brain enhancement techniques, such as integrating languages, visuals, and sounds, they were able to learn hundreds of new words in a single day, and, more importantly, retain them long-term with incredible ease.

One impressive result? After undergoing super brain enhancement, students were able to retain information 85% better than their peers six months later. That's a remarkable difference and a clear indicator that the methods being employed are not just gimmicks, they are backed by real science and produce genuine cognitive benefits.

At the schools where these methods are put into practice, the approach is holistic. Instead of enforcing rigid, traditional learning structures, students are encouraged to engage in whole-body relaxation techniques, promoting an environment conducive to learning. In these environments, students aren't stuck in one position; they have the flexibility to choose their chair, which helps create a more comfortable and personalised experience.

Once settled, soothing background music sets the mood, playing rhythmic, calming melodies to ease the mind. This gentle, relaxing atmosphere primes the students for more effective absorption of new information. This way, the traditional barriers to learning, stress, discomfort, and distraction, are removed, allowing the students' brains to function at their optimal level.

So, while it's easy to dismiss these techniques as "new-age" or "alternative," the reality is that they are empowered by sound research and have shown tangible improvements in learning and memory retention. This isn't just a passing trend, it's the future of effective education and cognitive enhancement.

Learning the Super Way: A New Era in Education

Brain enhancement techniques, already successfully implemented in various schools, are revolutionising how students learn. These methods combine relaxation, music, and innovative teaching tools to improve memory retention and boost learning efficiency. Unlike traditional methods, where students struggle to retain vocabulary or concepts, schools using brain enhancement solutions report up to an 85% improvement in retention over just six months.

In these progressive learning environments, students are not only taught traditional subjects but are also guided through practices that target the whole body and mind. By starting their day with soothing classical music, like baroque or largo sounds, students enter a state of relaxation. The rhythms of this music help synchronise both mind and body, reducing stress, lowering blood pressure, and regulating heart rate, all while promoting a shift from the high-frequency beta waves (associated with active thinking) to alpha waves (linked to calm focus and relaxation).

The results of such programs are not just anecdotal. Studies back the assertion that music, relaxation, and rhythm have tangible effects on cognitive performance.

The brain's ability to process, absorb, and retain information is significantly improved when students are in a relaxed and focused state. For instance, the act of listening to music alone has been shown to improve heart rate variability and enhance mental clarity. This relaxed state also helps students naturally absorb new concepts without the pressure of stress or fatigue.

But brain enhancement doesn't stop at the classroom door. These techniques also work wonders in helping adults, from business personnel to professionals, boost productivity and mental clarity. That's why many people invest in CDS, software, or online courses designed to enhance their brainpower. As the brain functions optimally, new skills are developed, leading to greater success in various aspects of life.

How Brain Enhancement Influences Student Attitudes and Performance

When students are placed in a brain-enhancing environment, the results go beyond academic performance. They begin to feel a sense of ownership over their learning. In schools that focus on accelerated learning and brain optimisation, students not only excel academically but also take on the role of ambassadors for change, inspiring teachers and peers alike. Their eagerness to learn motivates educators to seek new tools, methods, and programs to further enhance their students' abilities. This creates a positive feedback loop, where the enthusiasm for learning grows and spreads, benefiting everyone involved.

The Role of Parents in Brain Enhancement Success

As schools adapt to brain-enhancing techniques, the role of parents becomes increasingly vital. The collaboration between educators and parents has always been critical, but now more than ever, it's essential that parents understand the potential of these new methods. By embracing the concept of brain enhancement, parents can advocate for better educational tools not just for their children but for all students in the school.

In environments where success is expected from every student, parents shift their focus from simply ensuring the success of their own children to supporting the success of every child. They can become powerful agents of change by pushing for the adoption of brain-enhancing programs that foster an environment of growth, curiosity, and accelerated learning. Their involvement has a ripple effect, encouraging schools to continuously improve and adopt the best methods for nurturing all children's potential

The Role of School Staff in Supporting Brain Enhancement Programmes

While teachers and administrators are essential in implementing brain enhancement programs, other school staff also play a crucial role. Teaching assistants, cafeteria workers, school security, custodians, and bus drivers all contribute to creating a positive environment that supports relaxation and learning.

- **Teaching assistants** help shape the classroom culture and support students in staying relaxed and focused.
- **Cafeteria workers** ensure students have nutritious meals, which are essential for cognitive function.
- **School security and custodians** create a safe and clean environment, fostering a space conducive to focus.
- **Bus drivers** set a positive tone for the day, helping students mentally prepare for school.

When all school staff work together to create a calm and supportive atmosphere, brain enhancement programs become more effective, leading to better learning outcomes.

The influence of school staff on the brain enhancement community is significant because they help shape the overall school culture. Their attitudes and behaviours send a message to students about their value and role within the community, even beyond the classroom. Staff members, by supporting the brain enhancement program, contribute to:

- **Fostering a positive school environment**: The attitudes of staff members help students feel valued and supported, creating a culture where learning and personal growth are prioritised.
- **Serving as community conduits**: Staff act as key links between parents, students, and the school, ensuring communication and support flow smoothly. They play an active role in aligning with the program's goals.
- **Collaborating in the learning process**: In schools promoting accelerated learning, all staff members, teachers, administrators, and non-teaching staff, engage in a collaborative process, exploring assumptions about student needs and ways to improve the learning environment.

In essence, the actions and attitudes of the entire school staff contribute to making the brain enhancement program more effective and sustainable, as they reinforce the idea of learning as a shared responsibility and a community effort.

Office administrators are like the behind-the-scenes heroes of brain enhancement! They have the power to make a huge impact on how well students can absorb, retain, and grow in a learning environment. Here's how they can turn the tide for brain-boosting success:

1. **Budgeting for Brilliance:** Administrators control the purse strings, meaning they can direct funds toward the latest brain-enhancement tools, tech, and resources. They can ensure the school is equipped with cutting-edge programs that enhance learning.
2. **Curriculum Champions:** They don't just monitor; they can actively collaborate with teachers to introduce innovative brain-enhancement strategies into the curriculum. By championing new learning techniques, they help schools stay ahead of the curve in providing students with the best brain-boosting tools.
3. **Professional Growth Gurus:** Administrators can organise training sessions and professional development opportunities to ensure that teachers and staff are well-versed in the latest brain-enhancement techniques, making sure everyone's on the same page and using the most effective methods.
4. **Support for Special Needs:** Office admins can work with parents and special education teams to ensure that every child, no matter their challenge, has the tools they need to succeed. With the right support, no student gets left behind.
5. **Program Architects:** Whether it's launching a new learning initiative or expanding on a successful one, administrators are key in implementing programs that accelerate learning. They listen to feedback from parents and teachers, then make decisions that serve the best interests of all students.

6. **Advocates for Change:** On the state level, they are the voice for what works at the school level. They fight for policies that allow schools to continue improving and growing in their brain-enhancement practices.

Administrators at the top of their game are not just managing, they're driving innovation. They stay current on the latest curriculum and pedagogical advancements, ensuring their school remains at the forefront of educational development. But they don't keep these insights to themselves. Instead, they share their knowledge freely with teachers, staff, and school professionals, fostering a collaborative environment where everyone grows together.

By sharing the latest in brain-enhancement techniques and strategies, these administrators spark change not just within one school but across entire states. Their leadership and vision extend beyond the school walls, advocating for brain-enhancement programs and helping to spread these innovations to other educational institutions.

In this way, administrators play a critical role in advancing brain-enhancement initiatives, helping both their schools and the broader educational community thrive.

What is the flip side to this equation?

The flip side to the equation is that while administrators have the power to create positive change, they also wield the potential to unintentionally or intentionally cause harm. In an ideal world, superintendents and administrators are responsible for ensuring that funds are distributed fairly, particularly to schools serving low-income students. However, this doesn't always happen.

In many cases, there is an unequal allocation of resources, where certain schools, especially those in underprivileged areas, find themselves constantly short of funding. This imbalance often leads to inadequate learning environments, fewer opportunities for students, and a widening gap in educational quality between schools that can afford to invest in brain-enhancement programs and those that cannot.

Thus, while administrators have the potential to accelerate learning and foster growth, there's also a risk that their decisions, or lack thereof, could perpetuate inequalities and limit opportunities for students who need them the most.

ꙮ

8

BRAIN PROGRAMMING & ENHANCEMENT PRINCIPLES

The theories behind modern brain enhancement rest on a powerful idea that only recently entered mainstream understanding: the brain can be programmed. This does not mean the brain is a machine in the mechanical sense, but rather that it operates through patterns. Thought patterns, emotional loops, conditioned reactions, and learned beliefs all behave like mental programs. They repeat, strengthen, and eventually become the default setting of how we think and respond. Brain programming seeks to work with these patterns instead of against them. It combines neuroscience, psychology, and behavioural conditioning to help individuals reshape their internal responses so they are no longer driven by old habits or unexamined fears. The goal is not to force the mind into something artificial but to help it return to a healthier, more balanced pattern of functioning.

Brain enhancement tools often use rhythmic or repetitive stimuli such as patterned sounds, guided voice instruction, or structured audio environments. These methods take advantage of how the brain synchronises with external cues. Over time, the mind begins to follow the rhythm offered to it. This gradual alignment makes it possible to interrupt negative thought cycles and replace them with more constructive ones. When the mind is exposed repeatedly to calming audio signals, steady vocal guidance, or structured relaxation techniques, new neural pathways begin to form. These pathways support emotional regulation and help reduce tendencies toward anger, anxiety, and stress. Instead of spiralling into chaos during difficult moments, the brain becomes better at pausing, recalibrating, and choosing a grounded response.

A significant part of this work involves communicating with the subconscious mind. This is the part of the brain that holds deeply ingrained beliefs, automatic reactions, and emotional reflexes formed long before we were fully aware of them. The subconscious stores everything from childhood experiences to unexamined fears, desires, and interpretations of the world. It shapes how we behave even when we think we are acting rationally. Brain programming tools aim to reach this deeper layer. When repetitive sound patterns or guided messages bypass conscious resistance, the subconscious becomes more receptive to change. This is how individuals begin to break free from habits that once felt impossible to control, whether it is emotional overeating, persistent self-doubt, procrastination, or the urge to react impulsively when stressed.

These tools also support the development of positive characteristics. Confidence, calmness, focus, and happiness are not abstract ideas. They correspond to real neural patterns. When a person practices relaxation, focuses on gratitude, or repeatedly engages in positive self-directed thought, the brain rewires itself. Over time, the emotional centres settle, the prefrontal cortex becomes more active, and the overall system shifts toward a steadier sense of self. Practical results include a stronger ability to manage difficult conversations, better concentration during work or study, and a deeper sense of control during emotionally charged moments.

One of the most valuable aspects of this approach is goal-setting. Goals are often derailed not because people lack ambition but because their subconscious programming works against them. Someone may wish to wake up early, exercise, or avoid unhealthy cravings, but the mind defaults to older patterns whenever stress or fatigue appears. Brain enhancement methods aim to undo these lower-level loops so the mind is not constantly fighting itself. When the brain is reconditioned to trust new habits, reaching goals becomes more natural and less emotionally draining.

It is important to acknowledge that the brain ages, and with age comes a natural decline in certain cognitive functions. Reaction times slow, memory becomes less sharp, and emotional resilience may weaken. But the idea that this decline is irreversible has been disproven. Through deliberate stimulation, mental training, relaxation, and healthy neurological habits, the brain can regain clarity and strength even later in life. Brain programming tools offer a bridge between science and practice. They help individuals realign their thought patterns with healthier responses, allowing the mind to overcome ingrained habits, emotional triggers, and cognitive slowdowns.

In the end, the true power does not come from the tools themselves but from the mind that learns to use them. These methods work because the brain is capable of remarkable transformation when given the right environment, the right stimulation, and the right intentions. When individuals learn to guide that transformation consciously, they gain access to a sense of emotional balance, cognitive clarity, and personal empowerment that many assumed was out of reach. This is the promise of modern brain programming. Not artificial enhancement, but the awakening of capabilities that were always there, waiting to be strengthened and reclaimed.

ᘓᘐ

9

CRAFTING APPROACHES FOR BRAIN ENHANCEMENT

As people grow older, the brain starts to slow its processes. With increasing age, stress accumulated throughout one's lifetime causes the brain to diminish or fade. The brain's stability weakens, and it starts to fluctuate. This means that a diminutive stimulus could prove beneficial to the brain, since it uses the degeneration process to organise the brain to produce a stable structure. The brain can resist the most increased fluctuations and withstand more than humans can understand. The latest brain enhancer solutions have made it possible to transform the degenerated mind.

Brain enhancement recordings:

Modern brain enhancement programs have evolved to provide a wide range of features designed to cater to different needs and lifestyles. One key feature is the use of recordings that help with relaxation, enabling users to block out distractions and focus better, whether they're working, studying, or simply unwinding.

Many programs also offer "Wake Up" sessions, which provide a natural alternative to caffeine for starting the day with energy and focus. These sessions can help users feel more alert and ready to tackle their day without the typical crash associated with stimulants.

Customisation is a core feature of these brain enhancement tools. With the ability to adjust settings such as volume, pitch, and brightness, users can tailor the program to fit their specific needs. Whether it's for students, athletes, artists, or musicians, the flexibility of these programs ensures that everyone can make the most of them.

Additionally, some brain enhancement software integrates protocols that enable users to create personalised documents or action plans, offering a structured approach to problem-solving. This ensures that users are always in control, whether they're working on tasks or engaging with background sounds. The customisation options allow users to fine-tune the experience, helping them achieve their goals more effectively.

Brain enhancement scripts:

Scripts in modern brain enhancement programs are a powerful tool for personalising the user experience. By allowing users to customise their sessions, these scripts can be tailored to fit specific moods and needs. For instance, users can link to articles, background files, or exclusive member areas, all of which can support their brain enhancement journey.

One of the standout features is the "super tools for learning" found within the software. These tools offer control over brainwave frequencies, particularly alpha and theta waves, which are known to facilitate deep relaxation, focus, and creativity. By customising these frequencies, users can adjust the program to fit their desired mental state, whether it's boosting energy, motivation, or mental clarity.

The program also provides the option to adjust the length of sessions with customizable loops, allowing users to decide how long they want to listen to specific recordings. To ensure the best results, the program suggests that sessions be conducted in quiet, distraction-free environments, helping users fully immerse themselves in the experience. During the sessions, fade-in and fade-out phrases will appear, which are designed to guide the mind's ability to interpret and integrate the sounds, enhancing the overall effectiveness of the session.

By offering these personalised options, brain enhancement programs help users achieve their mental goals with precision and ease.

How the mind is relaxed:

The use of wave sounds targeting alpha and theta brainwaves is a key feature in brain enhancement programs. These calming sounds promote relaxation and help the user shift into a state of focused productivity, while simultaneously lifting their mood. The beauty of these techniques is that they allow users to keep their eyes open and continue working, yet still experience the soothing benefits of the sounds. The brainwaves, associated with deep relaxation and enhanced memory recall, transport the listener into a state reminiscent of childhood, where long-term memory feels more accessible and vibrant.

As the session progresses, a woman's voice gently guides the user with positive affirmations, repeating phrases that evoke feelings of motivation and excitement for life. This voice triggers emotional responses, reinforcing a sense of optimism and enthusiasm. The psychological basis behind this process is to induce a trance-like state, which enables the user to focus on positive emotions, rather than being bogged down by negative thoughts or stress. This shift in mental state helps to enhance concentration and mental clarity, promoting overall well-being.

Brain enhancement modality:

Brain enhancement programs today offer a wide array of modalities to cater to various learning and emotional needs. One of the standout features is the ability to choose visuals that can help users better visualise and understand their feelings, which enhances emotional intelligence. Kinaesthetic options are designed to improve users' ability to take action and connect their emotions with physical responses, boosting overall engagement and motivation.

The core goal of these programs is to enhance long-term memory, and they achieve this by providing hundreds of high-quality visual and audio sessions. These sessions can be easily exported to CDS or WAV-integrated systems for convenience. Users can also record their sessions using a microphone or utilise the 'Text-to-Speech' utility, which makes the process even more personalised.

Some software also offers dual inductions, a feature that simultaneously introduces multiple layers of stimuli to engage the brain more deeply. Users can fine-tune their experience by controlling affirmations, suggestions, scripts, and sound files.

For an added layer of immersion, some systems connect to Audio Strobes devices, combining sound with light for a more intense brainwave stimulation experience. Additionally, extensive ebook documentation helps guide users through the process of relaxation, serving as both a resource and a guide.

The beauty of these programs lies in their adaptability. They allow users to customise their brain enhancement experience based on their unique personality, cultural influences, and even genetic predispositions. This level of personalisation empowers individuals to program their minds for peak learning and performance, unlocking their full potential.

How Kinaesthetic features work:

Kinaesthetic features target sensations of the body's Range of Motion (ROM).

The sensations trigger perceptions or the sense of motion, including weight, position of muscles, tendons, joints and so on. The concept is to stimulate the nervous system and cells to ignite the brain to produce effectively. Kinaesthetic choices improve the way the user perceives and thus help in expressing feelings and taking action effectively.

Brain enhancement programs are like your personal mental coach, helping you level up in all areas of life. Whether you want to improve long-term memory, lose weight, build new exercise habits, boost your business skills, or just improve your creativity, these programs have got your back.

The magic lies in the combination of voice and sound. Let's say you want to start exercising but can't seem to get into it. These programs will play sounds and voice messages that remind you how much fun exercise can be, over and over again. Eventually, hearing these positive affirmations helps change your mindset, and you'll find yourself more motivated to get moving!

It's the same idea as breaking bad habits. Struggling to quit smoking? Daily sessions reminding you of the benefits of good health, healthy lungs, and the power of making positive choices will slowly help you kick that habit. With consistent use, these programs make it easier to replace old habits with healthier, more productive ones.

They also work wonders for improving social skills. If you're feeling a little unsure in social situations, listening to affirmations that encourage confidence and respect will boost your self-esteem. Over time, you'll notice how much easier it becomes to connect with others, whether it's with friends, family, or colleagues.

So, whether you're looking to transform your body, mind, or habits, brain enhancement programs offer a fun and engaging way to achieve your goals. The key is consistency, make it a part of your daily routine, and watch the magic unfold!

Enhancing memory power:

These programs work like a mental reset button, using repeated positive affirmations paired with soothing sounds to improve memory and relaxation. By listening daily, you're essentially training your brain to ease stress and absorb information more easily. The beauty of these programs is that they target different brain waves, alpha, theta, and even kinaesthetic responses, helping to enhance communication skills and brain functionality.

Alpha brain waves are key here. They help you relax and focus, which in turn boosts memory retention. The software uses neurofeedback (that's the voice and sounds) to trigger these brainwaves, sending helpful signals to your brain and body. This process enhances everything from creative thinking to cognitive skills and memory.

And there's a bonus: the visuals and sounds combined work like a time machine, taking you back to a child-like state where everything felt fresh and vibrant. When you feel younger, you feel more confident, and that confidence directly improves memory and overall mental clarity. It's like giving your brain a rejuvenating spa day, only, it's a daily ritual that pays off with improved focus, creativity, and memory!

Impact on improving willpower:

Brain enhancement programs are a game-changer when it comes to boosting willpower. If you're struggling with habits like smoking or drinking, these programs can be tailored to target both addiction and willpower. By combining the right audio tracks that promote relaxation and strength, the program helps you tap into a calmer, more empowered state of mind.

As the sounds relax your body and mind, they create a mental space where willpower can flourish. It's like giving your brain the room it needs to make better choices and fight those cravings. The more you listen, the stronger your resolve becomes, allowing you to break free from bad habits and build a positive, healthier routine. Imagine tackling your goals with renewed energy and determination, all because you gave your brain the tools to unlock its full potential!

Impact on boosting energy level and motivation:

There are options within these programmes that focus on boosting energy and motivation. Once a selection is made, find a quiet area to eliminate distractions. Keeping the eyes closed enables the user to get the most from the programmed sounds.

ഇന്ദ

10

THE POWER OF SELF-DIRECTION

There was a time when scientists believed that the deepest workings of the brain and body were entirely out of our hands. Electrical rhythms, chemical pulses, hormone releases, and shifts in heart rate were viewed as automatic processes that operated far below conscious influence. The human body was thought to be governed by internal machinery that acted independently of intention. People could observe their anxiety or excitement, but they could not alter the speed of their heartbeat, the flow of stress hormones, or the electrical activity of their brains. For decades, this belief shaped our understanding of what was possible for human performance.

That perspective changed with the arrival of biofeedback. Through a combination of sensitive instruments and real-time feedback, researchers discovered that people could, with training, influence systems that had previously been labelled involuntary. When individuals were shown their own physiological data as it occurred, they slowly learned to shift what seemed unshiftable. They could steady their heartbeat through focused breathing. They could lower their blood pressure by relaxing specific muscles. They could slow or even reshape electrical patterns in their brain simply by observing them and adjusting their focus or emotional state. What began as an experimental curiosity evolved into one of the most important discoveries in modern mind-body science.

Technological advances in the past several decades have amplified this potential. Devices can now track minute variations in brain waves, micro-fluctuations in skin temperature, subtle changes in muscle tension, and shifts in the body's stress response. Instead of guessing what their mind is doing, individuals can see it displayed directly through visuals, sounds, or interactive programs. The brain, which once felt like a sealed black box, becomes something that can be observed, trained, and strengthened through deliberate practice. This makes mental control tangible and measurable rather than abstract or mysterious.

When people learn to recognise the signals of their own mental states, they gain the ability to shift those states with far greater precision. A person who sees their brain slipping into unfocused patterns can redirect attention before drifting becomes a habit. Someone who notices tension rising can intervene long before stress takes over. Over time, the brain becomes more responsive, more balanced, and more resilient. This ability opens new doors in learning, creativity, and performance. Super-learning, the idea that individuals can absorb information rapidly or enter periods of heightened clarity, begins with the simple act of understanding and influencing one's mental landscape.

The concept of unlocking the brain's deeper capabilities remains a topic of debate, but the evidence continues to grow. Studies show that when individuals train their brain activity under guided conditions, they can expand memory capacity, enhance concentration, calm emotional storms, and improve their ability to shift between mental tasks. These changes are not magical or artificial. They arise from the brain's natural plasticity, which allows it to reorganise itself based on what it practices and what it repeatedly experiences. Biofeedback simply provides the mirror that makes this learning possible.

The most exciting part of this field is the shift in perspective it inspires. Instead of assuming that our mental abilities are fixed, we begin to see the brain as dynamic and responsive. Instead of feeling trapped in certain moods or patterns of thought, we learn that these patterns can be modified. Instead of viewing stress and distraction as unavoidable, we see opportunities for intervention and growth. The tools may rely on technology, but the transformation comes from within the mind itself.

In essence, biofeedback reminds us of something profound. We often underestimate the power we have over our own internal world. The brain holds far more potential than we tend to acknowledge, and with the right cues, feedback, and training, we can access levels of mental clarity, emotional steadiness, and cognitive strength that were once believed to be out of reach.

ജ്ജ

11

UNDERSTANDING BRAINWAVES

One of the most fascinating discoveries in modern neuroscience is the understanding that the brain communicates not only through chemical messages but also through rhythmic electrical patterns known as brainwaves. These rhythms shift depending on what we are doing, how we are feeling, and what our mind is trying to process. When we are deep in concentration, the brain vibrates at one frequency. When we daydream or relax, it slips into another. When we sleep, it enters still deeper patterns. These waves never turn off; they simply adjust like the dimmer switch on a light, guiding us into different mental states throughout the day. Brain enhancement tools build upon this natural system by using sound, rhythm, and guided audio to nudge the brain toward states that support memory, clarity, creativity, or rest. It is not about forcing the brain into artificial conditions. It is more like offering a gentle invitation that encourages the mind to settle into the exact state it needs.

Beta waves form the backdrop of our normal waking life. When we are alert, making decisions, solving problems, or focusing intently, beta activity rises. It sharpens awareness, fortifies concentration, and keeps us mentally active. When brain enhancement programs stimulate beta frequencies, the mind often becomes clearer and quicker, and tasks that once felt scattered become more manageable. For people who struggle with anxiety or racing thoughts, this might sound counterintuitive. Interestingly, well-guided beta stimulation can calm anxiety because it replaces chaotic mental noise with organised focus. It is similar to adjusting the lens on a camera. Once everything comes into focus, the strain decreases, and clarity feels natural rather than forced.

Alpha waves sit at the gateway between wakefulness and calm. This is the state most people drift into when they are relaxed but still aware, possibly daydreaming or imagining something that inspires them. Alpha waves open the door to creativity because the mind is both calm and receptive. It is not trying to perform. It is simply allowing ideas to rise to the surface. As people age, alpha activity often decreases, which can make relaxation feel difficult and creativity feel distant. Brain enhancement programs that encourage alpha waves help restore this natural rhythm. They offer the mind a rare chance to soften its edges, to drift comfortably, and to recover from the constant stimulation of modern life. When alpha activity is strong, it becomes easier to think intuitively, solve problems in fresh ways, and rest deeply without slipping into distraction.

Theta waves occur in states of deep relaxation, light sleep, or moments of profound calm. Many people feel a taste of theta when they meditate, when they drift off just before sleep, or when they lose themselves in a moment of insight. Theta is a unique state because it blends awareness with tranquillity. It slows the mind enough for emotional processing, creative breakthroughs, and memory consolidation. Many brain enhancement programs use theta frequencies to help users access a state where learning becomes easier, and the mind feels both present and peaceful. This is why theta training is often used for reducing stress, combating insomnia, or encouraging deep mental programming. When the mind is in theta, it becomes more receptive to positive suggestions and more capable of absorbing new information with minimal resistance.

Delta waves represent the deepest level of rest. They occur during dreamless sleep when the body is repairing tissues, balancing hormones, and restoring energy. Delta activity is essential for physical renewal, emotional stability, and long-term memory storage. People who struggle with chronic pain, migraines, or hypertension often find delta stimulation helpful because it encourages the brain to enter restorative sleep. When delta rhythms are supported, the entire body benefits. Many people wake up feeling lighter, clearer, and more balanced because the mind has finally been allowed to enter the healing space it desperately needs.

Alongside these patterns, many programs incorporate white noise or layered frequencies that produce a soothing, consistent sound. This mixture of tones may seem simple, but it plays a powerful role in stabilising the brain. White noise masks environmental distractions, encourages steady neural rhythms, and guides the mind into states that support relaxation or focus. For many users, it becomes the anchor that helps them release tension, settle their thoughts, and transition into healthier sleep cycles.

When these tools are used thoughtfully, the effects can be significant. People often experience improved focus, faster learning, more restful sleep, and reduced mental fatigue. The real purpose is not to artificially stimulate the mind but to create an environment where the brain can function at its natural best. Stress, overstimulation, and modern pressures constantly pull the brain out of balance. Brainwave training gently brings it back. It offers people the mental space they rarely find in their day-to-day lives. In this space, memory sharpens, thinking becomes clearer, and the mind begins to feel whole again.

Brain enhancement programs ultimately remind us of something simple but profound. The brain already knows how to rest, repair itself, and reach its full potential. Sometimes it only needs a bit of guidance to remember how.

ꕥ

12

NEURAL NETWORKS

Modern brain enhancement tools work on a deceptively simple principle. If you can support the structures that allow the brain to communicate, you can change the very quality of thought itself. The brain is not a single machine but a vast network of tiny electrical conversations. Every idea, every memory, every moment of clarity is created when one brain cell sends a message to another. When this system functions smoothly, life feels easier. When it slows or becomes overloaded, even the smallest tasks can feel like climbing a mountain. Brain enhancement solutions were developed to support this communication network and to help the brain process information with greater speed, clarity, and resilience.

At the heart of this process are the brain cells themselves. A single neuron can connect to thousands of others through delicate extensions called dendrites. These branches act like the listening posts of the nervous system. They receive signals, sort information, and ensure that messages flow from one area of the brain to another. For decades, scientists believed that the number of dendrites and the strength of their connections were fixed. We now know the opposite is true. Dendrites grow in response to stimulation. They can strengthen, multiply, and reorganise themselves when the brain is exposed to certain types of sensory input, sound patterns, and focused mental training. When brain enhancement programs stimulate these pathways, they encourage neurons to forge new connections and strengthen old ones. The result is a brain that processes information more quickly and responds more effectively to the complexities of everyday life.

Dendrites are more than biological structures. They are the physical expression of learning and adaptability. When they increase in number and activity, the brain becomes more flexible. It can hold more information at once. It can shift between tasks with ease. It can analyse situations without feeling overwhelmed. Brain enhancement tools support this process by providing stimuli that invite the brain to reach outward, grow new branches, and rewire itself in beneficial ways. This natural expansion is what allows people to think more clearly, respond with greater emotional balance, and tap into creativity that may have felt inaccessible before.

Alongside structural growth, these programs guide the brain into specific mental states by influencing its electrical rhythms. Brainwaves represent the language of the mind. Different frequencies correspond to distinct states of awareness, such as relaxation, concentration, problem solving, or deep rest. When a program introduces sound frequencies that match these rhythms, the brain often synchronises with them. This synchronisation helps users settle into calm when they are stressed, focus when they feel scattered, or remain steady when they are overwhelmed by sensory overload. It is not about forcing the brain into a mode it does not want. It is about reminding the brain of the natural patterns it sometimes forgets under the weight of modern life.

Sound plays a surprisingly powerful role in this process. The human brain responds instinctively to rhythm and tone. Certain sound patterns can increase alertness while others slow the mind into deep relaxation. Scientific studies have shown that sound can significantly improve the brain's ability to absorb and process information. Students studying with carefully chosen background sounds have demonstrated improvements in learning that reach more than fifty per cent. Verbal communication and comprehension also rise when sound is used strategically because the mind becomes more fluid and receptive. Sound reduces mental tension, softens internal noise, and allows the brain to shift into a state where memory, creativity, and comprehension feel more accessible.

When all of these elements come together, the effects can be transformative. Neural communication becomes faster. Dendritic growth increases the brain's capacity to manage complex information. Brainwaves fall into healthy rhythms that support focus, clarity, rest, or creativity, depending on what the user needs. For many people, this leads to better decision making, steadier emotions, quicker recall, and an overall sense of mental ease they may not have experienced for years.

What brain enhancement programs ultimately offer is a reminder that the brain is capable of far more than we often realise. It is designed to grow, adapt, and rebuild itself across a lifetime. When given the right stimulation and the right environment, it becomes not only more powerful but also more balanced and resilient. These tools do not take over the brain's natural abilities. They simply help the mind return to the state it always intended to inhabit: clear, focused, calm, and deeply capable.

ജ്ര

13

HOW PROGRAMS WORK

Mind Spa solutions are one of the most innovative brain enhancement products available today. These programmes use a mix of techniques to target specific brain waves like beta, alpha, and theta to promote relaxation and mental well-being. Here's a deeper look at how they work:

- **Brainwave Targeting**: Mind Spa solutions focus on adjusting the brain's activity through targeted frequencies. Beta waves are linked to heightened alertness and focus, alpha waves to relaxation and stress reduction, and theta waves to deep relaxation and creativity. These frequencies help guide the brain into different states that improve cognitive abilities, memory, and overall mental clarity.
- **Frequency Following Response (FFR)**: This technique uses rhythmic sounds and visual stimuli to synchronise with the brain's natural frequencies, promoting a relaxed state. The brain "follows"

the frequencies presented to it, leading to natural relaxation and enhancing mental functions.

- **Proven Benefits:** Mind Spa solutions have been shown to improve memory, cognitive thinking, problem-solving skills, and creativity. They help users concentrate better, boost their mood, and manage stress effectively. For people with conditions like Attention Deficit Disorder (ADD) or Attention Deficit Hyperactivity Disorder (ADHD), these programmes provide targeted support, helping to improve attention and mental organisation.

Biomedical techniques in brain enhancement often utilise biofeedback solutions, which are fascinating tools designed to help individuals gain control over their physiological processes. Here's a breakdown of how these techniques work:

1. **Biofeedback Mechanism**: Biofeedback involves using monitoring devices to measure various bodily functions, such as heart rate, brainwave activity, and muscle tension. By providing real-time data on these functions, biofeedback helps users become aware of their body's responses and teaches them how to control these processes consciously. For example, someone using biofeedback might learn how to lower their heart rate or reduce stress by calming their mind.
2. **Brainwave Modulation**: Biofeedback can target different brainwaves, such as theta waves (low frequency) and beta waves (high frequency), which are linked to different mental states. When a person experiences stress, their brainwaves can shift, creating a feeling of being "on edge." By using biofeedback devices, users can learn to regulate these brainwaves to achieve a more relaxed or focused state, depending on their needs.

3. **Engaging Tools:** To enhance the effectiveness of biofeedback, these programmes often incorporate music, puzzles, games, and other interactive activities. These tools not only keep the user engaged but also help stimulate brain activity in a fun and engaging way. For instance, solving a puzzle might help regulate the brain waves while offering a sense of achievement.
4. **Stress and Performance:** Biomedical techniques help individuals better handle stress by giving them the tools to recognise when their body is becoming tense or anxious. By using biofeedback to monitor and control these reactions, users can manage stress more effectively, improve mental performance, and even enhance their overall brain function.

Overall, biomedical techniques like biofeedback provide a hands-on approach to brain enhancement, giving users the power to influence their mental and physical well-being in real-time, making it a versatile solution for improving focus, relaxation, and overall brain health.

Biomedical tools: Watch Winder

The Watch Winder is an innovative biofeedback tool designed to help individuals remember important tasks and manage their daily routines. It's like a personal assistant right on your wrist, but without the need for a computer or phone. This simple yet powerful tool can provide gentle reminders for tasks like taking medication or remembering appointments. The watch can alert the wearer up to 30 times a day with either a vibration or a beeping sound, ensuring they don't miss a beat. It's equipped with 60 pre-programmed messages and can hold up to 30 personal messages, making it highly customizable for individual needs. Its large, easy-to-read screen ensures that people of all ages can benefit from it, especially those with visual impairments or seniors who may need extra assistance in staying organised.

The Watch Winder comes with two modes: Reminder Mode, which helps the wearer stay on schedule, and Training Mode, which is ideal for re-training individuals recovering from health conditions like strokes. This mode can help remind them to complete specific tasks, such as using the bathroom or performing rehabilitation exercises. The wearer can also choose between vibration or beeping alerts, offering privacy and discretion when needed.

In short, the Watch Winder is a versatile tool that enhances independence by ensuring people stay on top of their daily activities and health needs.

Watch Winders for ADD and ADHD patients:

Brain enhancement solutions are designed to help individuals with ADD and ADHD manage their day-to-day activities more effectively. One such tool, the Watch Winder, plays a key role in this process.

For those with ADD/ADHD, the watch serves as a gentle yet effective reminder of behavioural changes, alerting the wearer when something is off track. This immediate feedback helps users become more aware of changes as they happen, allowing them to adjust their behaviour before it escalates.

In cases where someone with ADD or ADHD needs to monitor and regulate their actions more closely, the Training Mode on the Watch Winder becomes invaluable. It offers structured reminders that guide the user to recognise when they are deviating from their tasks or behaviours, teaching them how to self-correct in real-time. This form of biofeedback can be especially useful in building self-regulation skills.

The Watch Winder isn't just for those with ADHD; it's also a great tool for anyone who has a medical condition requiring frequent reminders throughout the day. With its customizable features, like a stopwatch and countdown timer, this watch is also an excellent tool for teachers. It can help remind students when it's time to switch tasks, take breaks, or time themselves during tests, offering a structured way to stay on track. Whether for personal or educational use, the Watch Winder offers a practical and effective solution for improving daily organisation and task management.

Brain enhancement music:

Some brain enhancement solutions blend technology and music to help people relax and boost their cognitive abilities. Imagine a soothing soundtrack of wind chimes playing gently in the background, creating a peaceful atmosphere. This calming music works wonders in reducing stress and promoting relaxation, setting the stage for better sleep and mental clarity.

When the mind is at ease, it can focus more effectively, and memory retention improves significantly. Music that connects the listener with natural sounds, like the wind, ocean waves, or birdsong, has a profound effect. These sounds are proven to induce relaxation, making it easier for the body and mind to unwind and enter a state of tranquillity.

Both experts and schools are tapping into this therapeutic tool, recognising that combining nature-inspired music with brain enhancement strategies fosters a deeper connection with the environment. This connection not only promotes relaxation but also supports mental rejuvenation, helping people to focus, learn, and absorb information with greater ease.

How the sounds of music promote relaxation:

One unique solution in this category is the Sleep Mixer, which customises soothing sounds to help guide the mind into a relaxed state. By using sounds like drums, rainfall, seagulls, and ocean waves, this device creates personalised rhythms to enhance relaxation. The Sleep Mixer uses a specially designed gadget that allows users to mix and match different sound effects to suit their preferences.

The magic behind this tool lies in the Vibraphone technology, a percussion instrument with metal bars that produce calming vibrations when struck by small mallets. Underneath these metal bars are electronically motivated resonators, which amplify the sounds. The resulting music mimics natural elements like birds chirping, ocean waves, and gentle rainfall, bringing a peaceful ambience into your space.

These sounds aren't just for enjoyment, they actively work to reduce stress levels. The frequencies, combined with noise filters, help to drown out background distractions such as traffic or loud environments, promoting a peaceful atmosphere. By tapping into these proven sound-based techniques, the Sleep Mixer helps to ease anxiety and calm the mind, creating an ideal environment for relaxation, restful sleep, and mental rejuvenation.

ꕥ

14

LOCATING BRAIN ENHANCEMENT RESOURCES

The internet has completely transformed the world of brain enhancement. Only a decade or two ago, people relied mainly on books or occasional workshops to learn about memory improvement and mental performance. Today, any curious learner can explore thousands of tools and programs with just a single search. Entire ecosystems of digital libraries, online courses, downloadable programs, and multimedia solutions have emerged. Companies now offer everything from guided relaxation audios to stimulating brainwave sessions, and from visualisation videos to fully immersive cognitive training environments. Whether someone wants to sharpen their recall, regain mental clarity, or simply create a calmer internal state, there are countless solutions designed to meet those needs.

Online platforms make this exploration effortless. Typing in a phrase such as "memory improvement program" or "brainwave relaxation" instantly reveals a vast catalogue of products and services. Some focus on traditional techniques like guided meditation or breathing exercises, while others incorporate novel methods that blend music, art, sound frequencies, and visual stimulation into a single experience. Programs such as Mind Musicals, biofeedback systems, accelerated learning academies, and Mind Spa sessions have become increasingly popular. Their appeal often comes from the sense of convenience and personal choice they offer. People can now select the exact approach that fits their personality, learning style, and daily routine instead of settling for a one-size-fits-all method.

Yet technology is not the only path to a healthier, more capable mind. Many individuals seek balance through time-tested practices that have supported mental clarity for centuries. Techniques such as yoga, pranayama breathing, meditation, Tai Chi, and mindful stillness encourage the mind to slow down and reconnect with the body. These traditional practices are grounded in the idea that the mind performs at its best when the nervous system is calm and regulated. They help soothe stress, restore emotional balance, and encourage the brain to work with greater ease. For those who prefer a holistic, non-digital approach, these ancient methods continue to serve as powerful tools for cultivating long-term cognitive health.

The Healing Power of Music

Music holds a profound place in the science of relaxation. Long before modern medicine and sophisticated technologies existed, people instinctively turned to rhythm and melody to soothe the heart and steady the mind. Today, science has caught up with what humanity has always known. Music is one of the most natural and effective tools for calming the nervous system. Unlike medication, it comes without side effects, and unlike many modern interventions, it gently harmonises the mind instead of overwhelming it.

Listening to music invites the brain into a state of ease. When the mind becomes focused on soft, consistent sounds, it has a chance to let go of the mental clutter that builds up throughout the day. This process creates room for stillness. As the mind relaxes, the entire body follows. Muscles loosen, breathing deepens, heart rate slows, and the nervous system begins to reset. This shift into calmness makes it much easier for the brain to process information, encode memories, and store them effectively for later retrieval. People often notice that after spending time with calming music, they sleep better, wake with more clarity, and find it easier to remember things that once felt scattered or unreachable.

Music also strengthens the relationship between mind, body, and environment. It gently reconnects a person with their own emotions, with the rhythms of nature, and with the quieter parts of themselves. When this connection deepens, the mind becomes far less reactive. Stress levels fall because the internal world begins to align with a slower, more peaceful rhythm. Over time, this repeated exposure to calming sounds creates long-lasting changes in the brain. It cultivates a mental state where learning feels more natural, focus comes more easily, and information begins to flow without resistance. In this way, music becomes more than a simple pleasure. It becomes a powerful ally in cognitive health.

Accelerated Learning and Creative Brain Training

Accelerated learning programs build on the natural relationship between creativity and cognition. These courses blend music, drama, visual imagery, and storytelling to create an environment where learning feels alive instead of mechanical. They operate on the principle that the brain becomes more receptive when it is emotionally engaged. When students listen to calming music and follow along with spoken lessons or vivid visual presentations, their senses harmonise in a way that promotes memory retention and deep understanding. This dual sensory stimulation lets the brain relax and focus at the same time, a combination that opens the door to clearer thinking and stronger recall.

The methods used in accelerated learning are designed to awaken the playful, curious parts of the mind. Drama exercises activate imagination. Artwork stimulates visual processing. Storytelling enhances narrative memory. These elements reduce the pressure often associated with learning and encourage a sense of discovery. When the mind is relaxed, creativity rises, and information can flow in without resistance. Many institutions now recommend these programs because they not only improve learning outcomes but also reduce stress, increase confidence, and help students feel more connected to the material they are studying.

Research supports these approaches. Follow-up studies show that individuals who train with music, biofeedback, and creative exercises demonstrate improved concentration, deeper understanding, and greater emotional resilience. These programs do not simply offer techniques for memorising information. They help learners develop a healthy relationship with their own minds. The process becomes holistic. Students learn how to relax, how to engage fully with their work, how to balance effort with rest, and how to trust their brain's ability to grow stronger with practice.

Whether someone chooses digital programs, musical relaxation, or creative learning strategies, the underlying message remains the same. The brain is capable of extraordinary change when it is supported, stimulated, and given room to breathe. These modern tools and time-tested techniques offer different paths toward the same destination. They help people think more clearly, remember more effectively, and live with a sense of mental ease that carries them through the challenges of daily life.

ജ്ര

15

BRAIN ENHANCEMENT USER SESSIONS

One of the most fascinating developments in modern brain enhancement programs is the move toward deeply personalised sessions. Instead of offering a single method for everyone, these systems now allow users to choose the experiences that match their mood, intention, or personal challenge. If someone feels overwhelmed, they can select a session that supports stress reduction. If they feel distracted, they can choose a session that improves concentration. If they are seeking a spark of creativity, they can opt for a sequence designed to open the mind and awaken the imagination. This sense of personal choice shifts the entire experience. It allows the user to feel as though they are working with their mind rather than forcing it to behave a certain way.

Many of these sessions use a specific type of sound pattern that gently encourages the mind to return to a child-like mental state. This is not regression in the negative sense. Rather, it is a return to the openness, curiosity, and imaginative freedom that children naturally possess. When adults reconnect with that state, something beautiful often happens. Emotional blocks begin to loosen. Repressed memories, long buried under layers of stress, start to surface. Creative thinking becomes more fluid again. The mind, no longer weighed down, begins to recall with greater ease. It is almost as if the brain finally remembers how to breathe.

The auditory elements in these programs play a central role in this shift. Soft rhythmic patterns, warm tonal loops, gentle whispers, and carefully layered musical notes help refine the user's ability to communicate. The process does not just improve how a person speaks. It helps them listen. It supports better engagement in conversation and strengthens the ability to interpret subtle signals in social interaction. Sound, when used intentionally, becomes a tool that awakens emotional intelligence along with memory.

A defining strength of these programs is their capacity to adapt to the individual. They do not treat every user the same. Instead, they consider personality traits, cultural influences, and even genetic predispositions. A person from a music-oriented culture might feel more at ease with rhythmic affirmations. Someone who processes information visually may benefit from softer, atmospheric tones. Users seeking creativity receive sessions filled with repeated suggestions that affirm their imaginative abilities. With continued exposure, the repetition gently shifts the inner narrative, allowing the mind to replace doubt with possibility.

Customisation may be the most empowering feature of all. These programs often allow users to edit their own scripts, choose specific affirmations, or even build dual inductions that address two goals simultaneously. Some prefer direct statements such as "I am calm and focused." Others respond better to poetic imagery. The freedom to tailor each session makes the experience deeply personal and increases the likelihood that meaningful change will occur. When a person feels ownership over their growth, progress naturally follows.

Choosing Sounds and Finding the Right Fit

Since these programs draw from a wide range of cultural and psychological insights, the soundscapes they offer are equally diverse. Some tracks rely on soft flutes or rainfall, while others use warm vibrations, temple bells, or minimal atmospheric pulses. Users who want to explore beyond the presets can often browse online libraries and download additional sound files that match their emotional tone. This ability to experiment expands the experience. It helps each person discover the specific frequencies or styles that resonate most deeply with their nervous system.

Many programs offer trial versions, giving users a chance to explore the environment before making a commitment. These trials often come with limited features, but even with fewer tools, people can sense whether the overall framework suits them. The wide variety of choices available today makes it possible for almost anyone to find a solution that feels comfortable, intuitive, and aligned with their goals.

Do These Programs Really Work?

This is the question that often matters most. The honest and encouraging answer is that these programs tend to be highly effective when the user is motivated and consistent. Their success is not based on magic or mystery. They work by engaging alpha and theta brainwave states, stimulating the nervous system in a controlled environment, and guiding the brain toward patterns that support clarity, focus, and emotional balance. They also target deeper structures such as muscle tension, nerve pathways, dendritic growth, and cellular communication. When the entire network is supported rather than isolated parts, the brain can operate with greater vitality.

The central focus of these programs revolves around the synapse. The synapse is the tiny gap where one nerve cell passes information to another. It is the place where thoughts are born, where emotions take shape, and where memories begin. The more efficiently synapses fire, the more smoothly the entire mind functions. When programs target this level of communication, they are not simply promoting relaxation. They are restructuring the way the brain processes information, creating a foundation for sharper memory, calmer thinking, and more stable emotional responses.

The Central Nervous System plays an equally important role. When muscles, joints, tendons, and cartilage are tense or misaligned, signals can flow inconsistently. When they relax and open, communication becomes clearer. Effective brain enhancement acknowledges this relationship and incorporates tools that support both the mental and physical layers of cognition.

In the end, these programs work best when used with sincerity and intention. They are not shortcuts. They are invitations. They ask the user to engage with their mind, to trust the process, and to create space for change. When this happens, the results can be remarkable. The brain remembers how to function with strength. The mind begins to communicate more peacefully. The entire system learns to operate in harmony.

ജ്ജ

16

CORPORATE APPLICATIONS

Orientation programmes in many corporations today use a wide range of exciting alternatives to traditional training techniques.

Collaborative skills:

This collaborative skills workshop is an excellent blend of diversity celebration and brain enhancement techniques. The icebreaker activity, which uses scoring based on gender, job title, and professional experience, encourages participants to step out of their comfort zones. By prioritising diversity in team formation, participants are not only learning about the value of varied perspectives but also stimulating their cognitive flexibility, which is key in problem-solving and creative thinking. This type of brain exercise helps break down biases and fosters the development of new neural pathways by pushing individuals to think beyond their usual social circles.

After the icebreaker, the focus on team-building skills, such as conducting effective information-sharing meetings and brainstorming with soothing music, further enhances participants' mental agility and creativity. Music can act as a relaxing background, helping to reduce stress and improve cognitive performance. Through these activities, participants practice how to collaborate effectively, build trust, and manage change, all while supporting brain functions like creativity, memory, and communication. Incorporating such exercises into a workshop encourages not only professional growth but also personal development, as individuals learn how to navigate and thrive in diverse environments, which is essential for successful teamwork and innovation in any workplace.

The strength of diversity:

By emphasising diversity during orientation and ongoing training, companies are fostering an environment where creativity and innovation can thrive. Diversity isn't just about bringing people from different backgrounds together; it's about creating an atmosphere where different perspectives, experiences, and ideas can intersect and inspire new solutions, especially in research and development.

A workshop that focuses on mutual adaptation is a key element in ensuring that diverse teams function harmoniously and effectively. During such sessions, employees learn to appreciate the strengths each individual brings to the table while also developing the tools to navigate differences in communication styles, working preferences, and problem-solving approaches. This makes the transition into work groups smoother and encourages a culture of continuous learning and adaptability.

Moreover, when employees are empowered with strategies to adjust to work groups and understand how to maximise their collective strengths, they are more likely to contribute to creative and innovative solutions. This approach not only enhances productivity but also promotes a more inclusive and supportive corporate culture in which everyone feels valued, leading to higher engagement and long-term success.

Ending with a bang:

By encouraging new employees to take the lead in teaching others, you not only enhance their understanding of collaboration but also help them internalise key concepts. This method of teaching others as a way to reinforce learning is incredibly effective because it promotes active engagement and encourages individuals to think critically about the skills they are sharing.

Incorporating company executives into the team activities adds an extra layer of insight, offering employees a direct connection to leadership and providing a platform for cross-level communication. This connection can be especially meaningful in helping new employees feel welcomed, valued, and integrated into the company culture right from the start.

The activity that wraps up with reflection and the sharing of new ideas is also a great touch. It allows team members to solidify what they've learned, ensure that takeaways are meaningful, and create a sense of closure for the day. This closure is essential in helping participants feel that the time they spent together has led to tangible outcomes and strengthened team bonds.

Furthermore, the dynamic interaction between new and experienced employees is a great way to create a reciprocal learning environment. New employees bring fresh perspectives and enthusiasm, while experienced employees offer valuable guidance and mentorship. This blending of perspectives is invaluable for creating a culture of collaboration, continuous learning, and mutual respect within the company.

All in all, incorporating these elements into company orientations and team-building activities not only makes the experience more engaging but also lays the foundation for stronger, more effective teams moving forward.

ꕥ

17

THE ROLE OF TECHNOLOGY

What would it be like to use a machine designed for brain enhancement? Imagine sitting in a comfortable chair, pulling on a nice, lightweight version of some quasi-futuristic electrical headgear, hitting a small button within easy reach, then closing your eyes and drifting into a state of deep relaxation. Perhaps half an hour later, after shutting off the machine and removing the headgear, a better feeling prevails than before putting it on – a feeling of enhanced alertness and extreme lucidity.

This is because the brain, thanks to the influence of the machine, is now functioning far more effectively than it was before. The ability to memorise new information as well as recall what was previously learnt has dramatically increased. What's more, the creative thought process and problem-solving skills have expanded dramatically as well.

Optimising results from the use of a brain enhancement machine:

The idea of a machine designed for brain enhancement indeed sounds more like some crazy idea from a science fiction movie or fantasy novel, but the fact is that scientists have made efforts to develop just such a machine. A wide number of prototypes and theoretically functional models of brain enhancement machines are now in existence, and they are being used by ever-increasing numbers of people. However, awareness of the usage and efficacy of these machines among the public is still limited.

While scientists have been working on them for decades, they are still considered somewhat experimental. What's more, they operate by making use of certain capabilities within the brain that were comparatively recent discoveries, hence, they are not widely known outside the narrow field of research known as neuroscience.

The potential uses of a machine that functions by making the subject more clear-headed, quicker-thinking and in essence, higher-functioning, are certainly path-breaking and revolutionary. They may also be used by artists, novelists, painters and sculptors, who rely on their brains' abilities to function swiftly and with great creativity.

How does the general public react to the idea of brain enhancement?

Discoveries to do with the brain (including the promise of brain enhancement) offer individuals a greater insight into their personal emotions, thoughts, memories and, of course, intelligence. When scientists discover something new and exciting about the brain as an organ, the public in turn,have the opportunity to learn something new and exciting about themselves.

The general public is highly receptive to and even excited about the prospect of brain enhancement because the idea of the brain is one of great meaning, as it is something personal and completely private, and is intriguing. There is no place more private than one's mind. This is generally not the typical public reaction to anything produced from the field of neuroscience. Numerous discoveries have been made in a whole host of other fields as well – nuclear physics, math, biology, chemistry and advanced computer science, to name just a few. While these may have attracted limited attention, none of them have made quite the same sweeping impact as the advances in brain enhancement in the field of neuroscience. The general public is not so much interested in science as they are in the results of this discovery.

How does the excitement of the general public for brain research differ from that of scientists? The general public has attached a different and more appealing meaning to the concept of brain research. Perhaps they see it as an opportunity in the ultimate quest for self-discovery. Scientists, of course, do not feel the same sort of romance in their work; even if they did, they would still say they were objectively studying a physical organ. But we can conclude that the public is as enthusiastic as scientists are over the contribution that such a discovery makes to the whole field of neuroscience and brain research.

There are a variety of techniques devised by researchers that enable people to relax and so enhance their mental clarity to achieve the goal of brain enhancement. It is believed that humans are more likely to learn to alter old brain patterns and trigger brain patterns to new growth when they are in a 'non-ordinary' state of consciousness – a state which increases the brain's fluctuations. This conclusion may sound odd since it contradicts the accepted notion that learning is something that comes through practice and repetition, and that learning has a lot to do with conditioning.

In fact, it is a conclusion supported by research conducted in virtually every discipline of human studies. Educators, psychologists and other scientists of the brain are now exploring a variety of techniques to enhance the ability of both children and adults to learn, using methods such as drawing, guided imagery, meditation, autogenic, rhythmic breathing, singing, storytelling, dancing, music and relaxation.

Studies show that all these techniques can lead to dramatic increases in the ability to acquire, remember, and make creative use of information and ideas. The same studies indicate that such techniques can lead to dramatic alterations in brain chemistry and brain structure, as well as in human behaviour. The common denominator for these techniques is, of course, that each technique augments brain fluctuations by increasing brain-wave amplitude and/or by decreasing brain-wave frequency. There are a wide number of interesting studies that document the beneficial effects of boosting brain fluctuations, the purpose of brain and learning enhancement.

ഊഋ

18

MACHINERY IN BRAIN ENHANCEMENT

The discoveries surrounding machine-assisted brain enhancement have opened an entirely new doorway into human potential. For generations, the brain was viewed as a fixed and limited organ, impressive but bounded by biology. Today, that view feels outdated. Emerging science suggests that what most people experience as normal intelligence may represent only a faint outline of what the brain is truly capable of. Beneath the familiar surface lies an astonishing reservoir of power. The more we learn about it, the more we begin to realise that human cognition has depths we have not yet explored.

Over the last two decades, researchers have uncovered evidence that the brain operates in multiple states and rhythms, many of which can be shaped and strengthened through the right forms of stimulation. These findings challenge the belief that intelligence is static. Instead, they reveal a mind that can shift gears, accelerate, reorganise, and awaken dormant abilities when prompted by certain kinds of sensory input. The idea that machines might provide that stimulation is no longer speculative. It is becoming one of the most exciting frontiers in modern science.

As technology advances, machines designed to stimulate the brain have evolved from crude experimental devices into sophisticated tools capable of influencing electrical patterns, brainwaves, and neural pathways. Scientists are asking bold new questions. Can a machine expand memory? Can it improve focus? Can it increase intelligence? Can it help the brain access levels of performance that were previously considered impossible. With each study, these questions seem less hypothetical. The early evidence has already captured the attention of neuroscientists, educators, psychologists, and even sceptics.

Some of the earliest experimental users of these devices showed measurable changes. Their test scores rose. Their reaction times improved. Their ability to remember sequences, patterns, and details increased. They displayed heightened sensory awareness, faster recall, more synchronised brain hemispheres, and stronger, more coherent brainwave patterns. These results did not appear in every case, but they appeared often enough to reshape the scientific understanding of how adaptable the mind really is. Even those who doubted the technology could not deny that something unusual was happening in a subset of users.

The machines themselves vary widely. Some use pulsed light. Others rely on sound vibrations, rhythmic tones, or electromagnetic stimulation. Some are worn on the head, while others function through guided audio or visual sequences. The mechanisms differ, yet the underlying implication remains the same. The brain may be far more responsive to external stimulation than previously understood. It may be capable of accelerating its performance when given the right patterns of input. This realisation alone has transformed how scientists think about cognition, learning, and the boundaries of human ability.

For many researchers, the most compelling question is not whether one particular device works. The question is what these discoveries mean for humanity as a whole. If even a small number of these machines can reliably activate dormant capacities, then they reveal something extraordinary about the human brain. They suggest that our minds possess enormous reserves of intelligence, creativity, memory, and adaptability that remain largely untapped in ordinary life. They suggest that human potential is not a straight line, but a layered landscape with hidden levels waiting to be accessed.

This is why the field has attracted such passionate interest from inventors and innovators. The possibility that a device could enhance mental functioning is not just intriguing. It is revolutionary. The invention of writing transformed how humans store information. The invention of printing made knowledge accessible to millions. The invention of computers redefined how we think and work. A machine that could consistently increase cognitive capacity might stand beside these breakthroughs. It could alter education, reshape healthcare, redefine productivity, and expand the boundaries of personal development.

Of course, the science is still growing. Not every claim is supported. Not every machine delivers on its promise. But the direction is unmistakable. Modern discoveries suggest that the brain is not fixed at all. It is fluid, dynamic, receptive, and capable of being guided into states that unlock higher performance. These insights challenge old beliefs about intelligence and invite us to imagine what humans might achieve when we learn to work with the brain rather than against it.

If a reliable, consistent machine emerges that can enhance cognitive ability in meaningful ways, it could become one of the most significant innovations in human history. It would change not just how we learn or work, but how we understand ourselves. It would remind us that the human mind is not a finished product. It is a frontier. And we are only beginning to explore it.

ജ്ര

19

HOLISTIC ENHANCEMENT

The analogy of bodybuilding and strength training as applied to brain enhancement is a powerful way to understand the concept of improving mental faculties. Just as physical exercise targets specific muscle groups to build strength and endurance, mental exercise can focus on strengthening and enhancing specific cognitive functions.

Just like bodybuilders target particular muscles, you can focus your brain enhancement efforts on particular areas of cognition. For example, you might focus on memory improvement, creative thinking, problem-solving, or emotional regulation. Just as a weightlifter focuses on lifting heavier weights to build muscle, a person aiming for brain enhancement might choose challenging intellectual exercises or brain-training tasks to push their cognitive limits.

Devices and tools that aid physical strength, like barbells, treadmills, or cycling machines, have parallels in the brain enhancement field. Tools like brainwave entertainment devices, cognitive training apps, or neurofeedback machines can help stimulate and accelerate brain growth. They work by offering specific environmental stimuli (just like exercise equipment offers physical challenges) that encourage the brain to adapt, develop new neural connections, and improve cognitive functions. The cerebral cortex, as the seat of higher functions, plays a key role in this analogy. In evolutionary terms, the cortex is the result of our brain's ability to grow in complexity, allowing us to perform advanced tasks like learning, memory, problem-solving, and creativity. By stimulating the brain with the right kind of exercise (mental challenges, proper environments, and brain enhancement tools), we can enhance these functions. This kind of "mechanically induced evolution" through brain enhancement is akin to the way the human body has evolved to perform increasingly complex and efficient tasks over time.

Through brain enhancement, you can consciously target areas of the brain to develop, just as athletes target specific muscles to grow stronger. This targeted brain training can lead to improved mental capabilities, such as enhanced memory, faster learning, improved creativity, better problem-solving, and even emotional regulation, all of which are facilitated by the growth and strengthening of neural pathways in the cortex.

How does this relate to brain enhancement itself?

The scientific findings about the connection between sensory stimulation, particularly through music, and brain function are indeed profound. As the research suggests, the cortex, responsible for the higher cognitive functions of intelligence, memory, creativity, and emotional regulation, can undergo positive changes when exposed to enriching environments, such as music. The concept that intelligence can be enhanced by stimulating the cortex through targeted stimuli like music or other forms of sensory input aligns with the idea of neuroplasticity: the brain's ability to reorganize itself by forming new neural connections in response to learning and experience.

When students engage with music, as shown in studies, the results in terms of cognitive improvement are substantial. The evidence showing that music can enhance retention, math skills, verbal communication, and even IQ is compelling. This suggests that music doesn't just passively provide a pleasant background but actively stimulates the brain, aiding in both memory consolidation and brain activation across different regions. The improvement in IQ scores and cognitive abilities seen in the studies (including the Mozart Sonata experiment) suggests that music has the power to enhance both logical and creative thinking.

Moreover, the findings that music stimulates both the left and right hemispheres of the brain have important implications. The left side is often associated with logical thinking, language, and analytical tasks, while the right side is linked to creativity, spatial reasoning, and emotional processing. Music's ability to engage both sides of the brain supports the idea that it can boost a wide array of cognitive skills simultaneously, from reasoning and problem-solving to emotional regulation.

The link between music and emotional regulation is especially noteworthy. Music's ability to help individuals process emotions like anger, fear, stress, and sadness is a valuable aspect of its brain-enhancing potential. Emotions can often interfere with cognitive clarity, so by reducing emotional blockages and fostering relaxation, music can help the brain think more clearly and focus better. This is why music is often used in therapeutic settings to help individuals manage emotional responses and promote mental well-being.

In short, music as a brain-enhancement tool provides a dual benefit: it stimulates cognitive function while simultaneously promoting emotional balance, which together create a fertile ground for learning, memory retention, and overall brain health. By incorporating music into brain enhancement programs, individuals can optimize their mental faculties, from improved intelligence and memory to emotional resilience and creativity.

Musical software in brain enhancement

Technology has developed software with musical elements to help people relax. One of the latest solutions is neuro programming software. A user can download a trial version of this programme and use it for 30 days to test its ability to enhance the brain.

The user-friendly process is particularly notable: it begins with personal customisation, where users can identify their goals (such as PMS relief, stress reduction, or improving concentration), followed by selecting their emotional state or specific condition. This allows for a tailored experience, ensuring that users get exactly what they need at any given time, whether it's to focus on productivity, enhance creativity, or relax after a long day.

The integration of NLP (Neuro-Linguistic Programming) and Sensor Modality tests further personalize the experience, especially for individuals seeking to visualise or deepen their meditation. This step allows the software to select the most suitable methods to stimulate the brain based on the user's unique sensory preferences, improving the effectiveness of the program. The option to choose the duration of each session (20 or 30 minutes) provides flexibility for people with busy schedules, ensuring that even those with limited time can still experience the benefits of brain enhancement.

Additionally, the software includes practical features like the ability to export or convert the soundtracks into different formats (e.g., MP3) and energy-saving settings, making it convenient for users to integrate it into their daily lives. Addressing both the mental and environmental aspects of brain enhancement (e.g., quiet, distraction-free space), it helps users maximise the session's effectiveness.

Perhaps one of the most innovative aspects is its use of music. Music has long been known for its therapeutic benefits, and by combining it with biofeedback and personalised adjustments, the software leverages the calming and cognitive-enhancing effects of sound while also tailoring the experience to the user's specific needs. The program's capacity to address both the emotional and cognitive dimensions of brain enhancement makes it a comprehensive tool for improving mental well-being.

In summary, this neuro programming software goes beyond simple relaxation tools, offering a dynamic, user-centred approach to brain enhancement. It combines technology, music, and personalised feedback to support a wide range of cognitive, emotional, and psychological goals, empowering users to take charge of their mental health and brain function.

Brain enhancement options through music for the stressed-out workaholic:

Revolutionary software available today has taken relaxation to a completely new level. Technology has come up with solutions to help developers, writers, and those who constantly work long hours at a computer desk to find ways to relax the body and mind, enhancing the brain in turn. The programmes are ideal for relaxing while working.

These solutions combine music elements with flashes across the screen that guide the user into self-hypnosis and relaxation. At first, the impact from the flashing lights may be rather scary, especially if the user has traumatic symptoms, but once he/she gets used to them, they start to feel their mind go into a trance-like state.

Amazingly, the user does not go completely into hypnosis while working; rather, the mind starts to feel relaxed. Brain enhancement in such cases uses rhythmic electrical sounds repeatedly to draw the mind into relaxation. The entire process is simple, easy and safe. Download the software to the computer, hook up with headphones and relax. No one can hear the sounds. The aids improve memory and overall performance.

The calming effect of jazz music:

These programmes compose musical sounds to relax people in the same way that jazz relaxes the soul. During the '60s, jazz music took a turn, and the sweet sounds of smooth jazz came into focus. As jazz continued to grow, the bossa nova introduced by guitarist Charlie Byrd became a popular sound in living rooms around the world. Charlie played the saxophone with Stan Getz.

Jazz Samba, the first major bossa nova album, took off rather quickly, with electrifying sounds relaxing minds all around the world. While Mozart's music and ambient sounds fill the software, instruments, etc. that produce brain enhancement, one cannot forget that jazz made the statement when it came to relax the soul and mind. Smooth sounds in brain enhancement programmes are thus taken from the sounds of jazz that incorporate early jazz players, including Vivaldi, João Gilberto, Antonio Carlos Jobim, and so on.

Jazz uses ballets, salsa, tango, foxtrot, waltz, rumba and the bop to lift spirits, relax the mind and soothe the ears with electric rhythms, just as many other brain enhancement solutions do. Some other programmes make use of Brazilian tunes, ambient flows or sounds of horns.

Studies were also conducted on the brain's response to light, soothing voices, and this too led to the theory that brain enhancement, when combined with photic stimulations, voice, repeated musical sounds/voice, lights, etc., can help people reprogram the mind and find relaxation.

There are all sorts of people in the world – there are the creative minds, and then there are those who resist taking chances. There are also the people who dwell on past experiences, fearing the future and those who believe that they are always right. With so much positive and negative energy flowing in the world, it is no wonder that everyone is searching for answers to enhance their brains.

A characteristic of dissipative structures that is particularly important in our understanding of brain stimulation is that, for transformation or creation to take place, there must be either a lot of instability and fluctuation within the system so that even a small stimulus can bring about dissolution and reorganisation. Conversely, if the structure is stable, there must be some extraordinary influx of energy into the system, something powerful enough to destabilise a structure that is strong enough to resist most fluctuations.

The brain's ability to adapt, evolve and create:

The idea that greater instability in a system leads to more complex interactions, increased potential for transformation, and ultimately, greater wisdom, aligns with the theory of dissipative structures. In the context of the brain, this concept suggests that individuals who constantly engage in creative, artistic, or intellectual pursuits experience higher levels of mental fluidity, characterised by openness to new ideas and the ability to navigate chaos and turmoil. Far from leading to mental disorder, this continuous engagement with complexity and disorder can foster greater cognitive flexibility and growth.

The concept is grounded in the idea that the brain is not a static structure but a dynamic one, constantly evolving and reshaping itself. Creative thinkers and artists, who thrive in exploring new ideas and unfamiliar territories, often experience an increased neural density and a richer network of connections between neurons. This means that their minds can generate a broader spectrum of ideas, feelings, and intuitions, enhancing their ability to think creatively and solve problems.

Despite the apparent disorder that often accompanies creative thinking, it is through this very process of confronting and navigating complexity that higher-order thinking, wisdom, and innovation emerge.

This mental flexibility allows individuals to harness chaos as a source of growth, enabling them to adapt, evolve, and ultimately strengthen their cognitive abilities, including memory.

In essence, the greater the mental turbulence or complexity, the greater the potential for cognitive advancement. By engaging with these challenges, creative minds not only expand their capacity for innovative thinking but also enhance their memory and cognitive function, making them more adept at retaining and processing information.

What does this theory imply for people who are less creative and might resist innovation and change?

Ever met someone who just refuses to try anything new? Like, suggest a new restaurant or a different way to solve a problem, and they look at you like you've suggested jumping off a cliff. These are the folks who are *super* set in their ways. They treat every new idea like it's a suspicious stranger at their door. Instead of being curious, they filter everything through their past experiences, like trying to fit a square peg into the familiar round hole of their brain.

They're convinced they've got it all figured out. No room for doubt, no space for "Hmm, maybe I could be wrong." It's like their brain is a no-entry zone for anything unfamiliar. But here's the thing, our minds are supposed to be open systems. They thrive on new energy, fresh ideas, and the occasional mental shake-up. That's how we grow!

When someone shuts out anything new, they're trying to seal off their brain like it's Tupperware, airtight, untouched, and slowly going stale. And just like anything sealed too long, it stops being fresh. So if you want a brain that stays alive, curious, and vibrant, you've got to let the fresh stuff in, ideas, experiences, even a little uncertainty. That's what keeps the whole system buzzing.

Implications of efforts to turn the brain into a closed system: The idea of a closed brain is much like the idea of a cup of coffee that has gone cold or a static stone. Certainly, these closed systems are not threatened by chaos or disorder, but after all, who wants to have a near-equilibrium brain? Although this sort of brain, like a rock, would never be destabilised, it would also never have a new idea or feeling, either. It would lack so much of what makes the human brain special, unique and creative. In any case, physiologically, brains such as these normally have far fewer neural connections and much less developed cortical layers than the brains of people who remain open to and welcome the stimulation and natural energy of ideas.

ഇര

CONCLUSION

Brain enhancement offers many solutions to achieve guided relaxation and unlock the vast potential residing within each of us. Most programmes, instruments, courses, and techniques, whether employing electrical stimulation, music, or focused mental practices, aim to bring about relaxation and facilitate improved memory and cognitive function. Finding solutions to enhance our mental capabilities is something that increasing numbers of people are considering, driven by the desire to cope with a demanding world and realise their fullest potential. Since the brain signals the nervous system, sending and receiving messages to body cells, nerve cells, and influencing our brainwaves like alpha and theta, the prime focus in brain enhancement involves tools and methods that target these fundamental aspects of the human brain.

We have explored how biofeedback, accelerated learning, and a deeper understanding of our brain's functions can help individuals find what works best for their specific needs. The internet serves as a vast guide to solutions, offering customised effects, sounds, and voices. Reviews and shared experiences from those who have benefited from various brain enhancement products and training further illuminate the path. The latest programmes in brain enhancement often combine diverse approaches such as accelerated learning, yoga, mind-over-matter principles, specific sounds, and vocal guidance, using each method to target the brain from multiple angles. To enrich the overall experience, even practices like aromatherapy can be considered to increase the relaxation quotient.

In summary, the journey to an enhanced mind involves a combination of treatment, therapy, healing practices, and remedies. Psychoanalysis, combined with the strategic use of voice and sound, can help rehabilitate a mind that may feel degenerated by stress or age. With advancing age, and while navigating an increasingly demanding world, our minds can indeed feel the strain. However, it is the power residing within the human mind itself, when properly understood and stimulated, that holds the key to restoring what is lost and unlocking even greater capabilities. The path to brain training and conversion is an ongoing exploration, a commitment to understanding and nurturing our most complex and powerful asset.

ꕥ